Takefumi Aida

Buildings and Projects

Princeton Architectural Press

Princeton Architectural Press
37 East 7th Street
New York, NY 10003
212-995-9620
ISBN 0-910413-65-7

Printed in the United States of America
93 92 91 90   5 4 3 2
Production editor: Clare Jacobson
Book design: Kevin Lippert and Clare Jacobson
Special thanks to Sheila Cohen, Antje Fritsch,
Elizabeth Short, and Ann Urban.

Contents

Everything Not Revealed

Steven Holl

In the tradition of the Tofu Restaurant near Nanzen-Ji Temple, Kyoto, everyone gets the same courses; there is no ordering. The 350 year old restaurant serves only tofu—sesame tofu, tofu on sticks, boiled tofu, etc., but only tofu. In summer it is served on ice. As we sat in a 20 tatami-mat room on a cold January afternoon in 1986, Aida sketched on a napkin the concept of *oku*, or the "space that lies behind and beyond." Aida's diagrams of "Japanese space," layered space without a center, showed it to be clearly different from English picturesque or western classical space—the sense of mystery is everything not revealed.

My first encounter with the work of Takefumi Aida was to see, in the 1973 Rational Architecture Exhibition Catalogue, Annihilation House. The extreme simplicity of this white cubic house with its nearly windowless facade stands as a "zero" of "everything not revealed."

When I met Aida for the first time after a 1979 lecture in Halifax, Nova Scotia, we sat together for hours talking about an architecture whose driving beginning lies in concept rather than style. For ten years Aida's work has passed through "phases" of his own

design. Following the "toy block" phase, the hardest phase for me to accept, his work has now entered a "planar" phase organized around fluctuations. The *a priori* of a working compositional mode in Aida's architectural "phases" closes the vocabulary of his architecture which in some cases opens a range of meanings. The self-imposed limitations of planar composition achieve the most intensity in Aida's recently completed Tokyo War Dead Memorial Park for the 160,000 Tokyo citizens who perished in war. Rather than objectify the Memorial, deeply layered spaces create a "peace garden" spatially open-ended in every direction. The exposed concrete walls and gravel walks, the greenery and rolling planes of water, form an uneasy whole. Viewed in plan the two main groupings of parallel planes shuffle, a deck of cards in space, blurring the center. A walk through this inside-outside of shuffled layers is reformed by the movement of the sun's shadows. Intensity here is not in what we are looking at, for it seems neither landscape nor building. Here architecture must not appear. It is hidden, like a ghost in the clouds. It is in Aida's restraints that his work gains its meanings. The radical empiricism of Zen is reflected here in limitations, in a radical *a priori*.

From an "Architecture of Silence" to an "Architecture of Fluctuation"
The Work of Takefumi Aida

Botond Bognar

An 'invisible space' does not become visible unless it is consciously experienced and contemplated. The creation of space [thus should be], in a sense, entrusted to others: [the users and observers].

Takefumi Aida[1]

Takefumi Aida's architecture can be considered post-modern insofar as it has been, from the very beginning, derivative of architectural semiology and meaning, rather than simply of technology. Moreover, his designs, unlike those of the international modernists, touch upon the issue of tradition even if tangentially, along what may be called the delicately curving trajectory of a hyperbolic act. Then it is only curious that his early works, just as much as most of his later designs, are neither explicitly loquacious nor evidently meaningful and apparently did not seem to do much with traditionalism either; they were in fact moving toward an "architecture of silence," neutralizing rather than creating architectural form, or withholding rather than expressing meaning. In other words, they signalled the beginning of various paradoxical design intentions that have continued to imbue much of Aida's architectural *ouvre* until today. This mode of understanding and approach to architecture nevertheless aptly reflects much of the equally contradictory conditions within the Japanese urban developments and cultural landscape. These conditions became increasingly evident after the heroic and optimistic age of the 1960s, and also after the world-wide energy crisis and economic recession of the early 1970s.

Aida's debut on the architectural scene coincided with the "changing of guards" in Japanese architecture. In the 1970s a new generation of architects emerged and with it a new direction in design. Aida, together with several other designers (Minoru Takeyama, Mayumi Miyawaki, Takamitsu Azuma, and Makoto Suzuki) formed the informal group of ArchiteXt in 1971. As the name indicates, the group set out to investigate architecture as text, or rather, as language. In so doing, ArchiteXt responded to, as well as fostered, a new paradigm in architecture and urbanism. This paradigm, as opposed to the previous Metabolist architecture, was much more willing to accept the given reality of the Japanese city. Taking this reality as its point of departure, Archi-

1. Takefumi Aida, "From Toy Blocks to an Architecture of Fluctuation," *The Japan Architect* (June 1987), p. 203.

teXt favored "small scale interventions" rather than overall or radical replacement of the whole system.

Metabolism, the ruling architectural ideology of the 1960s, reached its epitome at the Osaka Expo-70, a grandiose showcase event that demonstrated, interestingly enough, not only Japan's tremendous technological advancement, but also the serious limitations of architecture and urbanism derived primarily from technology.[2] Metabolist architects, such as Kenzo Tange, Kiyonori Kikutake, and Kisho Kurokawa (the last representatives of Japanese high-modernism) regarded technology and industrialization as key agents for solving the problems of the fast escalating urbanization of the evolving new megalopolitan areas in Japan. Using large-scale and often utopian schemes based on megastructures and megaforms, these architects approached the city "from above" and tried to restructure it in a radical manner. They recognized the city simply as a rationally programmable artifice with an explicit emphasis on inventing and manipulating operational and organizational systems.

The next generation of architects, equipped with a different sensibility and concern, became critical of the Metabolists' self-proclaimed role as demiurge and tried to acquire an unpretentious perspective of social and urban issues. The new understanding advocated by this generation was actually a close approximation of the viewpoints of ordinary citizens living within the *existing* city. In this sense ArchiteXt was the first group to promote a counter-Metabolist or post-modern architecture in Japan. Also, they were among the first architects to openly acknowledge the influence and expression of paradoxes in their work. And in fact, like the architecture of its architects, the group itself was a paradox. ArchiteXt, at its first and only exhibition in Tokyo, issued no joint memorandum or manifesto; these architects followed no common line. Indeed, with their individual approaches, they aimed exactly at the opposite, emphasizing the multiplicity of expression within the language of architecture.

Takeyama outlined the "common" philosophy of ArchiteXt as "discontinuous continuity," referring undoubtedly to pluralism as a basic stance of the members.[3] Along with the paradoxes in their works could be found elements of humor, irony, etc. These designers were the first to introduce such notions as "pop architecture," "defensive architecture," "vanishing architecture," "polyphony in architecture," and what Aida called the "architecture of silence"

The megastructure of the Spaceframe over the Festival Plaza, at the Osaka Expo-70, was designed as a "prototype" for a futuristic "technopolis" or a "city in the sky." Architect: Kenzo Tange.

The Structuralist vision of a new city over the sea; Plan for Tokyo, 1960. Architect: K. Tange. Photo: courtesy K. Tange.

2. Most buildings of the Osaka Expo-70 were conceived as high-tech industrial products. In fact, many of them were designed by the members of the so-called Metabolist group: Kisho Kurokawa, Kiyonori Kikutake, Masato Otaka, and Arata Isozaki, with Kenzo Tange as chief designer. The layout and infrastructural organization of Expo, and most especially the steel super-structure of the Spaceframe over the Festival Plaza, were, in many respects, modelled after the new and technology-inspired urban visions of their designers.
3. Minoru Takeyama, quoted in Charles Jencks, "ArchiteXt and the Problem of Symbolism," *The Japan Architect* (June 1976), p. 21.

into contemporary Japanese architecture.[4] Thus, their buildings, with practically no exception, were unique dashes in the urban environment; their intended meanings and conveyed messages differed significantly from architect to architect, making ArchiteXt a representative sample of the whole New Wave of Japanese architecture that unfolded through the 1970s. The fact that the "group" had hardly come into being when it stopped functioning as a group, and has remained ever since an informal gathering of friends, further characterizes the new attitude toward paradoxes.

It became evident that responding to the changing qualities of the Japanese city required a much more complex and, to some extent, even "problematic" design strategy than what Metabolism and modernism, with their rather single-minded approaches to the issues of urbanization, were capable of advancing. The changing urban qualities manifested themselves in various and too often opposing directions. On the one hand, rampant modernization (the "modernist project") of industrial and technological progress, replaced the traditionally ambiguous and more flexible, resilient urban fabric with rigidly rationalistic and uniform new urban structures. In addition, this modernist project rapidly began to reveal other negative effects, the "dark side" of progress: congestion, increasing hazards, noise, pollution, alienation, etc. On the other hand, yielding to the imperatives of post-industrial "information" or consumer society, commercialism penetrated urban life and culture and converted virtually the whole built environment into commodity, a flood of constant stimuli with a "sensory overkill." The city became, as Hajime Yatsuka observed, a "sea of signs" with a flood of advertisements.[5]

The paradoxical developments of the Japanese city were of course similar to those that determined the course of urbanization in other late-capitalist societies, with one notable difference. These developments in Japan were much faster and the symptoms more acute than anywhere else. The reasons can be attributed partially to the pace of Japan's miraculous progress after World War II, and partly to the predisposition of certain social, cultural, and urban traditions in Japan. Such traditions include, among others, the Japanese predilection for change and impermanence. For lack of traditions of plazas or piazzas, the Japanese acquired a devotion to streets, street architecture, and a maze-like and ambiguous quality of urban "structures," to say nothing about a penchant for signs and symbols, which later prompted Roland Barthes to call Japan an *Empire of Signs*.[6] All of

Representative of Japanese "pop-architecture"; Niban-kan Building, Tokyo, 1970. Architect: Minoru Takeyama.

Modern urban district; new housing blocks in Kyoto's Yamanashi area. Photo: courtesy Ohbayashi Gumi Co. Ltd.

4. Takefumi Aida, "Silence," *The Japan Architect* (Nov.-Dec. 1977), p. 52.
5. Hajime Yatsuka, "An Architecture Floating on the Sea of Signs," in B. Bognar (ed.), *Japanese Architecture*, Special issue of *AD* (5/6 1988), p. 7.
6. Roland Barthes, *Empire of Signs* (Richard Howard, trans.), New York: Hill and Wang, 1982 (1970).

these traditional traits could in fact be easily vulnerable, if not conducive, to consumerist exploitation and devaluation.

The reactions of the new generation of architects to this rapidly unfolding dismal state of affairs were varied yet equally indicative of the dilemma and the limited possibility of architecture. Many New Wave architects retreated from the city and took up explicitly anti-urban positions with and within their small but unusually provocative designs. In this respect, the works of Tadao Ando, Toyo Ito, and Kazuo Shinohara are the best examples. Within ArchiteXt, Miyawaki was the one who sympathized most with this attitude. He noted: "We are now in a season, in which we must do all we can to protect from [the] outside."[7] Others, like Minoru Takeyama, Arata Isozaki, Fumihiko Maki, etc., explored the possibilities of new ways to communicate with the increasingly confused and "meaningless" built semantic context in which their buildings were inescapably set. Isozaki swiftly moved toward a highly conceptual mannerism; Maki developed a line of contextualism based on his notion of "group form"; Takeyama pioneered a somewhat abstract populism.[8]

Aida, an advocate of these avant-garde directions, responded to the overwhelmingly senseless visual noise of ruthlessly manipulated meanings of consumerist urbanism; he deliberately shifted toward another kind of architectural meaning and communication that could only emerge, paradoxically, within the realm of "silence." This realm of silence thus had nothing whatsoever to do with the muteness of the universal technological modernism. Yet, by the same token, it was even further removed from the jaded stylistic eclecticism of mainstream post-modernism upheld primarily by American neo-realists such as Robert Venturi, Robert Stern, and Charles Moore. If this is so, then where could the realm of this "nowhere-land" be found? What distinguished it from its counterparts, from its multiple opposites?

The answer seems to point in the direction of a paradoxically "negative" or in-between realm that curiously not only divides but, perhaps more so, connects opposite phenomena. It goes without saying that at its core, such a realm very closely approximates the notions of void (*mu*) and absence (*ma*), the central theses of traditional Japanese thought and culture. Concealed expressions and highly controlled emotions make the Noh drama, the tea ceremony, the flower arrangement, and even the ambiguous disposition of architectural spaces the most poignant representatives

Cityscape in Tokyo's Shinjuku district.

Top: House with Territory-delineating Walls, Ashiya, 1977. Architect: Tadao Ando.
Bottom: House on a Curved Road, Tokyo, 1978. Architect: Kazuo Shinohara.

7. Mayumi Miyawaki, "In the Season of Protection," *The Japan Architect* (July 1977), p. 54.
8. Fumihiko Maki, "The Theory of Group Form," *The Japan Architect* (Feb. 1970), p. 39.

of the art of silence. This silence therefore is by no means dumb; it is a "many-voiced" silence. Aida himself wrote: "Architecture of silence must be pure. Within pure forms there must be [a] multiplicity of meaning . . . silent spaces are not seen with the eye; they are felt with the heart."[9]

In his first building, An Artist's House in Kunitachi, Tokyo (1968), Aida already manifests many of the characteristics and concerns he would put forward in his architecture of the early 1970s. Although the design includes a free-standing cylindrical staircase, symptomatic of numerous Metabolist projects, the articulation of the House's three simple geometric elements foretells Aida's later toy-block house designs, wherein architectural form becomes rather "incidental."[10] The two cubic and one cylindrical blocks, lacking any special emphasis on technology, are combined in a manner that is a clear deviation from modernist norms. The House features an atelier that appears somewhat as a "displaced space," with a degree of formal uncertainty, on top of the residence. The separately defined and handled elements, a kind of architecture-by-parts, thus all together provide an only "provisional" arrangement on the site. As Chris Fawcett observed, this "house-in-the-city . . . isn't comfortably honed down to a 'controlling centre' with 'assistant elements'; each part is shown to be something in itself."[11] The overall expression thus becomes withdrawn as if experiencing what Aldo van Eyck called "the clarity of a labyrinth."[12]

Before investigating further the issue of part-and-whole relationship, Aida became involved in the definition of entities or elements wherein the "uncertainty" of spatial and formal expression could prompt the viewer to be more actively engaged with architecture and, by extension, the built (urban) environment. An Artist's House in Kunitachi, and to some extent the Nirvana House and Annihilation House (1972), are representatives of what Aida calls the "space of encounters." He writes: "The very space I have been seeking is one born of a meeting between varying threads, one that produces an exalted tension as a result of that meeting."[13] One may say that Aida's "spaces of encounters" are spaces without their ordinary or normal credentials, spaces that necessitate repeated interpretation. By so doing, they acquire a *phenomenological* rather than objective dimension.

Both the Nirvana and Annihilation Houses, as indicated by their names, manifest a blankness of expression that is akin to the emo-

Kitakyushu Municipal Library, Kitakyushu, 1975. Architect: Arata Isozaki.

Hillside Terrace Apartments, Tokyo, 1969-76. Architect: Fumihiko Maki. Axonometric drawing.

Fountain of the Piazza d'Italia, New Orleans, 1978. Architect: Charles W. Moore.

9. Op. cit. 4.
10. The cylindrical shaft, both a sole means of vertical circulation/communication and a vertical structural support, was a very common design element in Metabolist architecture. The best example of this remains Kenzo Tange's Yamanashi Communications and Press Center in Kofu (1966), in which a total of 16 such shafts were incorporated.
11. Chris Fawcett writing on Aida's architecture in Muriel Emanuel (ed.), *Encyclopedia of Contemporary Architects*, New York: St. Martin's Press, 1980, p. 19.
12. Aldo van Eyck, "Kaleidoscope of the Mind" in A. van Eyck, *Miracles of Moderation*, ZGrich: ETH, 1978, p. 3.
13. T. Aida, quoted in Chris Fawcett, Op. cit. 11.

tionless facial expression of Buddha statues, symbols of ultimate nothingness or nirvana. And indeed, a closer investigation of the front elevation of the Nirvana House may yield the discovery of a "chirpy smile," which is both there and is not there. In this architecture only the subtle shades of silence can stir minute yet "telling" differences. In other words, Aida's designs of "silence" are the ultimate expressions of what can only be suggested but never fully said, or, as Fawcett remarked, they are "token hints of the 'eternal in the here and now.' "[14] Hereby then we are returned to a silent, non-formal tradition of Japanese culture, which in Aida's works takes shape without any nostalgic reversion to traditional forms and their literary meanings. Therefore these works can also be regarded as critical commentaries on the present state of architecture, an architecture that is increasingly obsessed with communication but is now capable of informing society about hardly anything more than its own succumbing to fashion, trivialization and commodification.

In the unprecedentedly volatile urban realm, Aida, similar to many of his peers in the 1970s, attempted to initiate a different kind of architectural discourse that could somehow remove architecture from the apparently inevitable process of being converted into another consumerist "object of desire." Kenneth Frampton was accurate in suggesting that representatives of "the Japanese New Wave, with their acute awareness of change and fragility, have become preoccupied with the precise definition of architectural entities or 'archemes'—that is, with phenomenological 'nouns,' which by virtue of their precise definition may be used to expose form to the unpredictable play of changing action."[15] Nevertheless, the notion of "silence" in Aida's architecture can take various "forms" and expressions. One of them is the simplicity of surface geometry, which is often assigned a unique role, something like that played by a Noh mask. This is already evident in the Nirvana and Annihilation Houses, yet it guides the design of the House Like a Die even more explicitly, so much so that the building borders on the absurd. Aida himself writes: The "House like a Die expresses the independence of architecture and the multiple meanings of dice . . . chance, gambling, suspicion, whiteness, cubical form, and so on . . . The idea of suitability of form . . . it ought to be one of the aims of architecture to overthrow [this] concept."[16] And he goes on: "[This] House presents itself as an ironical expression with a mask that is a die. The die is a huge face turned to the exterior space. It is a mask of architecture."[17] One may say that architecture itself is concealed behind this mask.

An Artist's House in Kunitachi, Tokyo, 1968. Architect: Takefumi Aida.

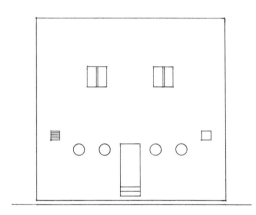

Nirvana House, Fujisawa, 1972. Architect: T. Aida. Elevation.

14. C. Fawcett, Op. cit. 11.
15. Kenneth Frampton, "The Japanese New Wave," in K. Frampton (ed.) A New Wave of Japanese Architecture, IAUS Catalog 10, New York: 1978, p. 3.
16. T. Aida, "Speculation in the Dark," The Japan Architect (Nov. 1972), p. 101.
17. T. Aida, "Silence" in K. Frampton (ed.), Op. cit. 15, p. 14.

In other cases Aida pushes this concealment, as a form of "negative" communication, even further, assuming the notion of an architecture of disappearance or "vanishing architecture." This is precisely what was intended in the PL Institute Kindergarten in Tondabayashi. The Kindergarten seems to be designed in the form of an ancient imperial burial mound; the building is a flat, reinforced concrete pyramid that "disappears" under the earth and grass that cover it. Architecture itself here has vanished, becoming but a formation of nature. The unusual, even absurd exterior then covers an interior (which is more appropriate to the world of children) organized around a central courtyard and playground. The intention of returning architecture to nature characterizes Aida's small Hotel at Shiobara as well.

Although some aspects of these buildings may appear similar to certain traditional forms, i.e., the burial mound, they are only incidental. Aida explicitly points out that the emphasis here is *not* on the form but on the process of suggesting the transitory nature of architecture. Thus he writes: "To make architecture disappear, or to pursue architectural beauty in the process of weathering and returning the building to nature, is my intent . . . In the case of the kindergarten of the PL Institute . . . the process of weathering has become important [while] in the case of the pension-style Hotel at Shiobara, . . . the conformity of the pitch of the roof to the incline of the topography, or the use of curved walls conforming to the natural contour, [is most essential]."[18] Nevertheless, it is important to emphasize that the issue of Aida's return to nature also means a defensive position, a rejection of the man-made environment, or the city.

Aida continues his attempt to neutralize architectural form, along with its "suitability" to the purpose of the project, in the Stepped Platform House (1976), resulting in another "silent" but also absurd building. Yet this House is, to a certain degree, already a transitional building in his works of architecture. Similar in shape to the Kindergarten yet covered with black tiles, the symmetrically designed small structure erodes at its ends and fragments into stairstepped profiles. These stairs, obviously leading nowhere, not only signal a literal "end of the road" and a metaphorical end of Aida's "speculation in the dark" (as he himself refers to his preoccupation in the early 1970s), but also imply the beginning of a new direction and phase in his design investigations.[19] From here on, "silence," although not completely abandoned, gives way to another, more cheerful theme—the notion of "play." The broken

PL Institute Kindergarten, Tondabayashi, 1974. Architect: T. Aida.

Stepped Platform House, Kawasaki, 1976. Architect: T. Aida. Section.

18. Ibid.
19. T. Aida, Op. cit. 16.

forms of the Stepped Platform House thus reappear in an altogether different disguise (or is it another mask?) in the fragmentary compositions of his Toy Block House series, the first one of which was completed in 1979.

The changing course in Aida's architecture, as much as in that of many others at the end of the 1970s, revealed some serious limitations of privatized architectural languages to communicate in the public realm of the city. Although the "autonomous symbolism" (as Charles Jencks called the phenomenon) of these languages might have had the special appointment to rehabilitate the language of architecture and generate a more meaningful architectural discourse than modernism had, it eventually failed to establish a common basis for such discourse.[20] These architects had to realize that they were actually adding to the Babel of architectural languages and to the increasing meaninglessness in the consumerist city. In other words, they were, paradoxically, promoting what they were determined to prevent, and so a need for a change in strategy arose.

Moreover, as the economic crisis slowly levelled off and a new environmental consciousness arose in Japan, architects started to look at the city not only as a place to confront or a place to escape from, but also as a place with plenty of untapped resources and potentials for creativity, and, as such, a realm worth coming to terms with. Several aspects of the fragmentary, chaotic, and even anarchic quality of the Japanese city came to be interpreted as progressive features to be implemented in individual architectural works.[21] As the architect Fumihiko Maki noted, the Japanese city is "an environment that is fragmented but that constantly renews its vitality precisely through its state of fragmentation."[22] Thus, as architects started to respond to this unique and fast developing man-made environment with renewed and heightened sensibility, the latently preserved flexibility, vital energy, and resilience of the oriental Japanese city came to be rediscovered. The 1980s witness a most dynamic, new stage in urban architecture, often labelled as a "new renaissance of urbanism" in Japan. And in this unfolding new renaissance the boundaries between creative (poetic) and critical processes dissolve.

Aida's Toy Block Houses are the result of a similar understanding. They grow out of those conditions that the contemporary urban scape presents to its observing citizens; they dramatize, perhaps also parody or criticize, these conditions. The return of the archi-

20. C. Jencks, Op. cit. 3, p. 24.
21. This is especially conspicuous in Kazuo Shinohara's recent architecture which, according to him, is inspired by "Tokyo: The Beauty of Progressive Anarchy," in K. Shinohara, "Chaos and Machine" in *The Japan Architect* (May 1988), p. 28.
22. Fumihiko Maki, "Spiral," *The Japan Architect* (March 1987), p. 33.

tecture-by-parts, though in a reinterpreted fashion, has now yielded both a fragmentary quality more akin to the urban environment and a sense of playfulness, which is easier for anybody, especially children, to identify. Nevertheless, the idea of an "architecture as toy" is not completely new in Aida's work; it can be traced to many of his previous projects. "Architecture as toy" can be found, interestingly enough, in a unique, traditional design method of Japanese carpenters, the so-called *okoshie* drawings, which Aida often employed in his first period of "silence." In this mode of both design and architectural perception, the various planar elements of a building—floors, ceilings, exterior and interior elevations—are laid out as surfaces in one composite plan similar to the paper pattern that small children cut before folding and gluing it into a three-dimensional form like, say, a die. This was precisely one of the ideas behind the House Like a Die wherein the configuration and number of windows coincided exactly with the marks of a die.

Yet the Toy Block Houses make up an altogether different set of toys by complying with the rules of another "game." Within these buildings, usually small private residences, the architectural components are articulated as the simplest geometrical solids—triangular and rectangular prisms, cylinders, stepped forms, etc.—which thus are virtually identical throughout the series. Using this method, the houses are put together so that these formal as well as often structural elements retain their own recognizable identities, like those of the various compositions that children build from the same set of toy blocks. In this way, the world of children, elements of traditional Japanese architecture (particularly the Shinto shrine), and rational Western architecture are equally represented in the images of these houses.

Furthermore, Aida's toy block projects allude to a new form of urban architecture inasmuch as the blocks can be regarded as elementary formal units that, in their multiplicity, comprise the urban landscape. If so, Aida's design operations do have an implicit affinity to those of Aldo Rossi, the Italian architect and theoretician; Rossi's urban design enterprise first fragments the architecture of the traditional city into its formal types, then reassembles it into a contemporary, rational artifice. Rossi's procedures are generally known as architectural or rather urban typology, and also as European contextualism. Aida's work at this time reveals the Italian master's influence; the early Toy Block Houses, such as the ones in Hofu (1979) and Yokohama (1980), are rationally or-

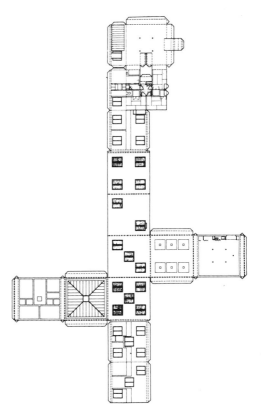

House Like a Die, Izu, Shizuoka Prefecture, 1974. Architect: T. Aida. *Okoshie* drawing.

Toy Block House No. 2, Yokohama, 1980. Architect: T. Aida.

dered and meticulously symmetrical designs. Symmetry and the
adherence to rational compositions, however, soon gave way to
more asymmetrical and apparently more scattered or "disor-
dered" compositions responding better to the "context" of the
Japanese city. In fact, some of them, like Toy Block Houses IV
and VIII, appear outright ruinous. At the same time, Aida gradually
made the size of the blocks smaller to look more and more like toy
blocks.

Cemetery of San Cataldo, Modena, 1976-86. Architect: Aldo Rossi.

The toy blocks were, of course, the visible aspects of these buildings as they appeared, more often than not, from the outside.
Moreover, while the exteriors of these Houses were overly con-
trived rather than spontaneous, the inside spaces remained rather
ordinary. Aida admits this in a candid self-criticism by saying:
"What was visible was all calculated, and I left as little to chance
as possible. Although I talked of the 'playfulness' of toy blocks,
that idea seemed gradually to have less to do with the spatial
composition of the buildings. I wondered if 'softer' toy block
spaces could not be devised. The focus of my concern shifted
from [the] 'visible' . . . to [the] 'invisible.' "[23]

After completing the tenth of his Toy Block Houses in 1985, a shift
in focus introduced the third, that is to say present, period in
Aida's architecture. An increased interest in the two-dimen-
sionality of thin wall planes and other surface-like elements in
parallel disposition replaced his preoccupation with the three-
dimensionality of solid blocks. Aida, acting as an "urban guerilla,"
openly exploded his own toy blocks and the architectural castle
he had built out of them to create not only houses for his clients,
but also a theory of legitimation for himself. This was certainly a
rare, although not unparalleled, act from an established, interna-
tionally acclaimed designer. The purpose here was to move
toward an architecture less restrained by the laws of three-dimensional compositions. Thus, again paradoxically, Aida evoked a
more profound sense of depth in space, while bringing the actual
buildings closer in nature to the contemporary Japanese urban
scape comprised overwhelmingly of a sea of thin layers: signs,
ads, architectural or other elements, etc.

With regard to his new intentions, Aida wrote: "One must give
primacy in design to vertical planes . . . To put it somewhat
abstractly, what this process involves is the fragmentation or scat-
tering of dimension . . . The result is neither entirely two-dimensional nor entirely three-dimensional. I choose to call it 2.4-

23. T. Aida, Op. cit. 1.

dimensional . . . The layered planes endow the building with depth. A similar effect is produced when one looks at an urban landscape through a high-powered telescopic lens. The buildings pile up and seem to fluctuate."[24] We should now obtain our own "telescope" and focus it not on the urban landscape, but on Aida's new "architecture of fluctuation." In so doing we may observe several features that, on the one hand, distinguish this architecture from other contemporary intentions, and, on the other hand, make it similar to them.

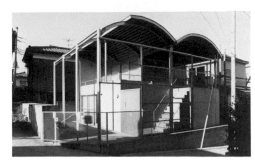

House in Magomezawa, Chiba Prefecture, 1986. Architect: Toyo Ito.

Today the tendency to conceive architecture as a field of multi-layered planar elements (walls, screens, fabrics, lattice works, etc.) is rather widespread in Japan. It reflects a vibrant sensibility that is induced by and comments upon the fragile and theatrical nature of the contemporary Japanese city, and, further, it underscores a general feeling of the "impossibility for anything [in our age] to reach a state of completion on its own."[25] Experience and understanding not quite unlike these seem to be at work in Aida's recent designs. Like the latest works of such architects as Hiromi Fujii, Hiroshi Hara, Kunihiko Hayakawa, Ryoji Suzuki, and even Toyo Ito and Itsuko Hasegawa, they are attempts to render the boundaries between architecture and the city, and/or between architecture and nature, "indeterminate." In these cases architecture is defined not as a complete, solid, and self-centered entity but, as much as possible, as the coincidental, sometimes even accidental, intersection of various elements, forms, "fragments," and signs, as well as "traces of events." By way of such disposition, these elements actually layer rather than contain architectural space in multiple or ambiguous ways that, all together, precipitate a realm of perceptual uncertainty in terms of boundaries, forms, meanings, etc. Furthermore, the buildings of some designers like Ito, Hasegawa, or Riken Yamamoto, because of the extensive use of light-weight materials (thin steel frames, perforated aluminum panels, wire mesh screens, teflon fiber fabric, etc.) gain a certain insubstantial or ephemeral quality.

Aida, in contrast to the architects above, and similar to Ando, Fujii, Hayakawa, and many others, employs reinforced concrete, a heavy and substantial material, almost solely in his buildings. Therefore, overcoming the limitations that materials and structural constituents set on an "architecture of fluctuation" (which is also a kind of "immaterial evocation of building") entails a more difficult and paradoxical job than in the above cases. Achieving the goal of "fluctuation" thus can only be ap-

24. Ibid.
25. Ryoji Suzuki, "An 'Archipolitique' of Architecture," *The Japan Architect* (Nov./Dec. 1986), p. 10.

proximated by way of subtle procedures working toward a "perceptual dematerialization" of architecture, making the layered planes as permeable or perforated as possible, while simultaneously exploiting their surface quality or "surfaceness."

It goes without saying that all of these intentions, including Aida's new designs with two-dimensional planes, are also informed by the similar traditions of Japanese art and architecture. According to these traditions, space—natural or built, depicted or actual—was always perceived and created as a "heterogeneous labyrinth" structured by layers of elements (rows of buildings, ridges of mountains, etc.) or, in the house, evoked by the multiplicity of thin, mobile, and translucent wall panels. Such ambiguous disposition of the constituent elements, which eschewed the fixating rules and effects of Western perspective, was conducive to a uniquely profound sense of depth or a phenomenology of space, regardless of its usually very limited or shallow physical dimensions. Thus, to better understand the "architecture of fluctuation," it may help, as Aida says: "if we think in terms of images: a *shoji* on which are cast the shadows of trembling leaves, the vague mist clinging to the foot of the mountain, a *sumie*-like landscape, the forms and sounds of ripples, each one slightly different."[26]

Aida's recent investigations in architecture have already yielded a considerable number of interesting projects whose qualities have an extremely sophisticated appeal. Therefore, he should be credited for having achieved many of his intentions. Nevertheless, some of his built works also reveal that Aida has yet to find his optimum means of execution. It seems that the more "restrictive" the function and/or the larger the size of the building, the more difficult it is, at present, to break down the structures into "fluctuating" walls. The GKD Building attests to this observation; it is actually conceived of highly conventional floor plans and interior spaces. Only the elevations are, or could be, arranged as layered planes, and even there, to a limited degree only. Thus, in the GKD Building, Aida's intentions exhaust themselves in more or less a kind of surface decoration within or in front of the exterior walls, balconies, etc., with an effect less convincing than in other works.

Much more successful are the smaller residential projects like the Kazama and Kajiwara Houses (1987). Here the parallel, reinforced concrete walls effectively penetrate the whole realms of the buildings and are able to loosen the constraints of closed, three-

26. T. Aida, Op. cit. 1.

dimensional volumes into a more fluid spatial entity. The articulation and perforation of the concrete walls, alternating at places with steel and frosted glass as well as punched aluminum panels, allow several interior courtyards and other small outdoor spaces to be incorporated into the porous fabric of architecture. When the "random" openings through the parallel walls visually overlap, they focus on various events both inside and out, filtering and blending interior and exterior worlds in a fragmented yet highly poetic way, akin to the poignancy of the sharp "snap-shots" of verbal expression characteristic of the *haiku*, a form of traditional Japanese poetry.

Aida's most successful recent project is the Tokyo War Dead Memorial Park, which is both a peace park and a monument completed in 1988 to honor the 160,000 Japanese from Tokyo who died during the war. Most of the walls here are freestanding, gate-like passages; they are arranged along two axes so as to inter-penetrate and conflict. Reflective surfaces, light and shadows, partial and fragmented vistas, plus the view and sound of water complement the architectural rendering and the range of experience. All together they inscribe on the site as well as in the human awareness a unique path that threads its way through a continuous realm of in-between, the thin and elusive borderline be-

Kazama House, Kawaguchi, 1987. Architect: T. Aida. View from the nearby Buddhist cemetery.

tween inside and outside, architecture and nature, permanence and transitoriness, existence and non-existence, or life and death.[27] The space, shape, and significance of this path are bound to remain silent, invisible, and inaccessible until the visitor embarks on the journey of experience and contemplation and, by so doing, partakes in their evocation. The Memorial Park, wherein his notions of silence, play, and fluctuation seem to come to a full circle, is certainly one of the most phenomenal and memorable designs in Aida's work to date; it no doubt makes us look forward to the further developments in Aida's architecture.

Botond Bognar is an architectural photographer and professor of architecture at the University of Illinois, Urbana-Champaign. He is the author of numerous publications, including the books *Contemporary Japanese Architecture* (New York, 1985) and *Japanese Architecture* (Special issue of *AD* 5/6 1988). Currently he is working on another volume to be published in 1990. Professor Bognar lived in Japan for several years and is also a correspondent for *A+U*, Tokyo. All photographs in this essay, except p. vi (b) and p. vii (b), are taken by B. Bognar.

27. Aida himself refers to many of these pairs of dual opposites in his "Architecture, Fluctuation, and Monument," *The Japan Architect* (Feb. 1989), p. 20.

Memorial Park, Tokyo, 1988. Architect: T. Aida.

Projects

1 9 7 2 — 1 9 8 8

Toy Block House 0 (Aida Block)

1 9 8 1

Aida Blocks are intended to be an aid to understanding
and composing architectural spaces. They can be used
seriously or playfully. Considering the shapes, one might
wonder what sort of forms could be created with them;
one experiences feelings of both anticipation and
uncertainty—as if opening Pandora's box.

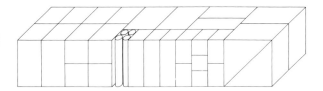

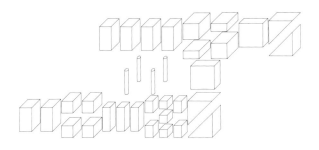

Aida Box

1 9 8 1

These blocks are meant to be assembled rather than piled one on top of the other. One table, four chairs, four storage units, and one lighting fixture fit into a one-meter-square box. The design takes into account ease of transportation.

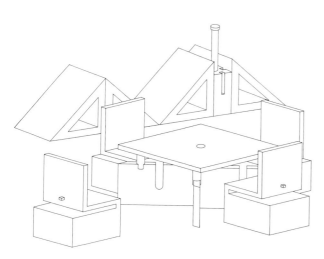

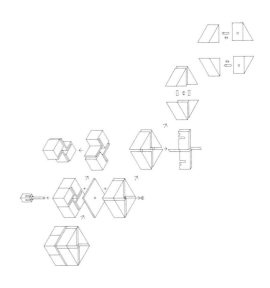

Toy Block House I

1 9 7 8

Like a child's building blocks, the rectangular solids that house the dental clinic on the first floor and those that accommodate the living spaces on the second floor are placed in parallel sets at right angles to each other. Glass blocks fill the openings placed in the building-block composition of the exterior forms. A desire to underscore the building-block forms determines the grooves rather than the exigencies of concrete pouring.

For the sake of symbolic recall, forms used outside the building are repeated inside. For instance, on one side of the house a post rises from the ground toward a concrete form at roof level in imitation of the ridge-supported post (*munamochibashira*) employed in ancient Japanese architecture. A similar post and trianglular solid are part of the structure of the house within the house—the cork box—which encloses the dining-room space.

 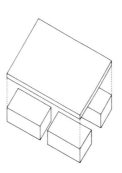 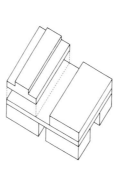 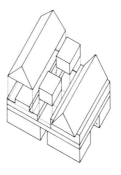 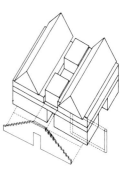

West facade.

View of east wall.

Cork box housing the dining room.

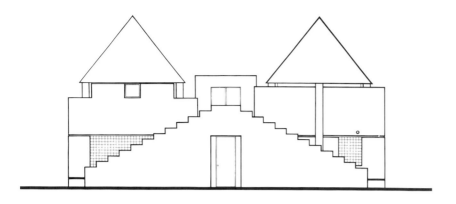

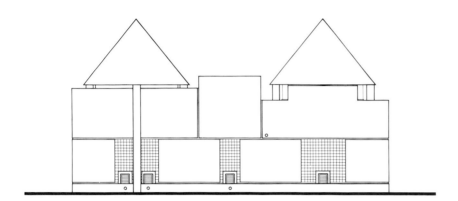

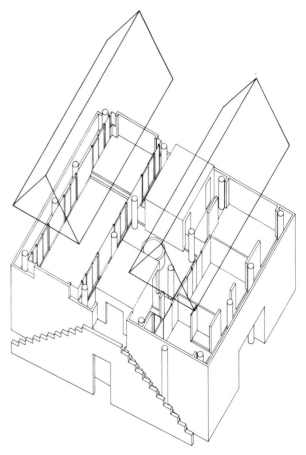

Isometric.

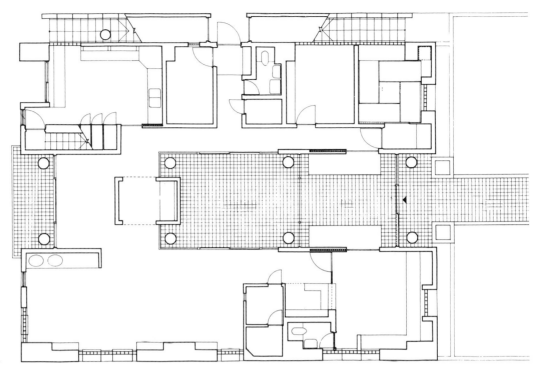

First floor plan.

Second floor plan.

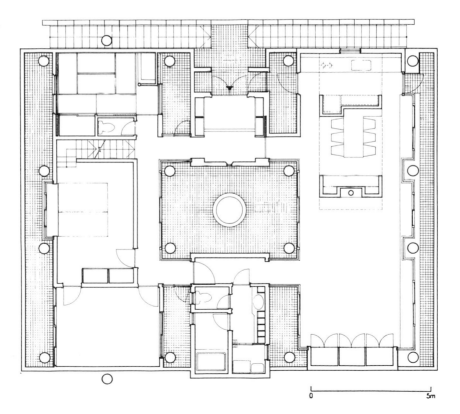

0   5m

Toy Block House II

1 9 7 9

There are an invisible method and a visible method of employing toy blocks. In the former, a block represents a unit of spatial composition. With the visible method, blocks are used literally as toy blocks; an analogy is suggested between whatever toy blocks are represented and a given configuration of blocks.

The visible method used here attaches "toy blocks" to the surface of a cubical box. Toy Block House II is a mixed-use building in a commercial area; consequently its facade is particularly important. Rather than give the inside and outside the same "toy block" expression, the design attempts to express the feeling of toy blocks merely through surface treatment.

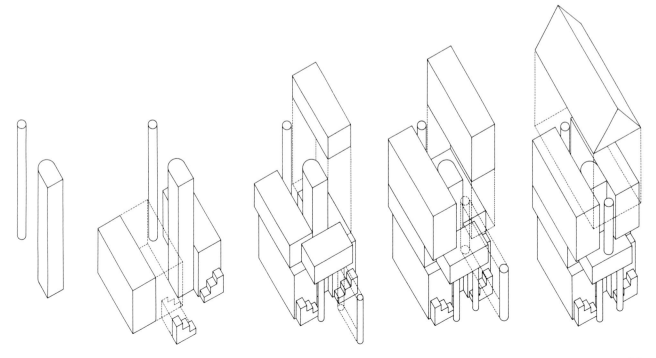

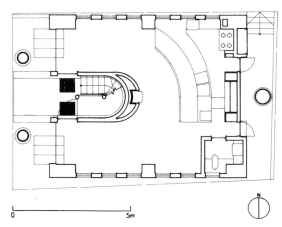

First floor plan.

West elevation.

Toy Block House III

1 9 8 1

Toy Block House III attempts to shift from an architecture of "hard" forms to one of "soft" forms. "Soft" architecture comes into being when an ongoing process of change is halted at some point. The process is very much like the process of playing with toy blocks—one continues to alter the configuration until the time comes to a stop, and at that moment a certain arrangement is fixed.

Using the toy block metaphor, I could halt the process of design at a point short of "completion," and by that means endow the architecture with a soft quality suggesting movement. One can pile the blocks in as many layers as one desires, and the layers become an expression of the time that is passing. Architectural design becomes a matter of connecting the fragments that have been piled in layers. As with all play, there are rules for playing with toy blocks. There are two basic modules, 600 millimeters for the interior and 1,200 millimeters for the exterior. There are obvious differences of scale between an actual building and a form made of toy blocks; in Toy Block House III, I reinforced this perceptual gap in some cases and disguised it in other cases, thus increasing the fictional character of the house.

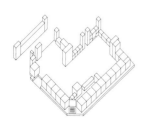 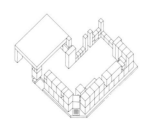  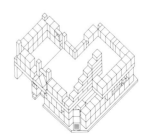

Colors are effective in creating the image of a pile of blocks arranged randomly or given an impression of disorder. The 600 millimeter pieces are given primary colors, and the rest are made either white or gray. The arrangement of the white and gray pieces is determined by numbering every piece in an elevation and then using a randomly numbered chart to select the coloring.

Architecture is the product of highly polished sensibilities. The value of architecture is determined by how well you represent your sensibilities through your work. We might say that, "Everything is play or not play," or that, "Everything is frivolous yet serious." We associate dualities with playing with toy blocks—construction and destruction, stability and instability, life and death.

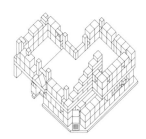
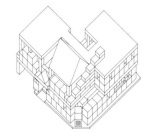
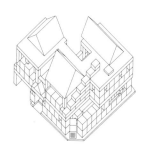

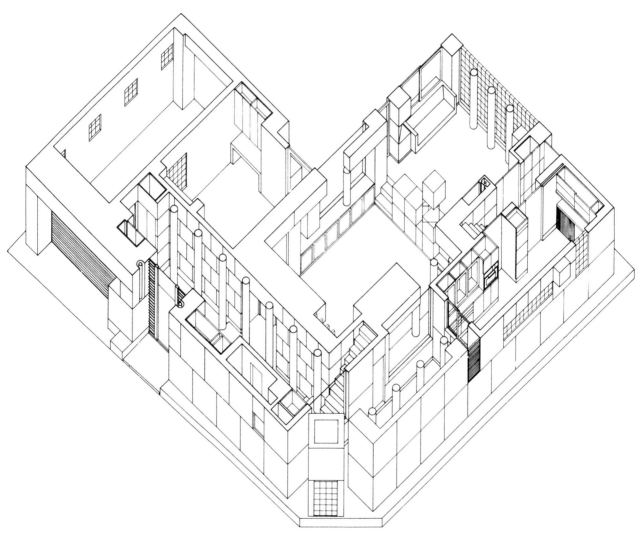

Axonometric.

First floor plan.

Second floor plan.

South elevation.

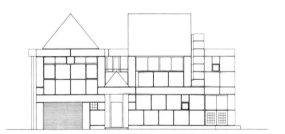

East elevation.

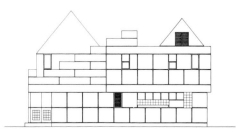

North elevation.

West elevation.

Opposite page
Top: view of north-east corner.
Bottom: view from the inner garden.
This page
Left: aerial view of east side.
Below left: detail of entrance.
Below right: interior of *tatami* room.

Toy Block House IV

1   9   8   2

Toy Block House IV is inspired by the idea of placing toy blocks in a box and then creating cracks in its surface to expose the blocks. I had this idea because of the character of the environment in which the house is situated; a concrete wall that suggests a box for toy blocks guards the house from the surrounding neighborhood and helps maintain a favorable living environment within. This is a composite structure of concrete for the wall (resembling a box made of cardboard) and wood for the individual rooms (or "grains").

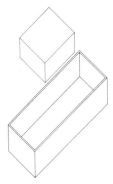 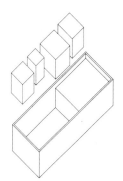 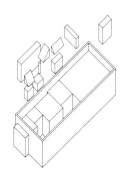 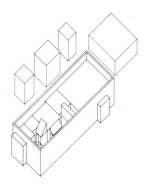

This house suggests the process by which a cardboard box is emptied and then refilled. There are many rules and restrictions in architecture such as building codes, circulation patterns, and structure; discrepancies exist between these conditions and the rule followed in playing with toy blocks (i.e., the rule that the blocks must be returned to the original box), and consequently there is a certain unpredictable element in the design.

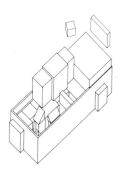 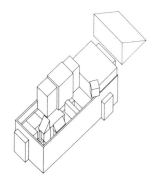 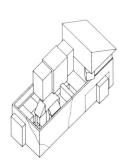 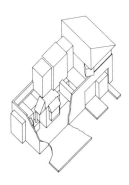

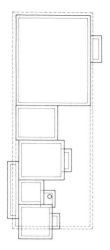
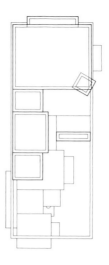

Block plans.

First and second floor plans.

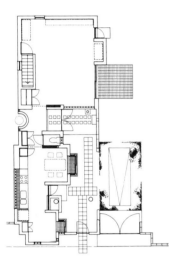

0   5m

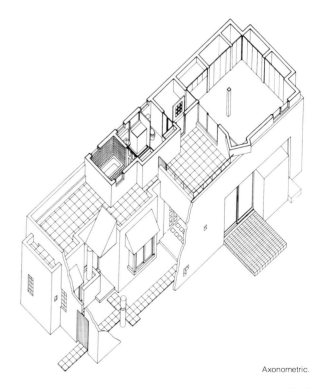

Axonometric.

Right: south entrance to court.
Below: view of east wall and court.

Toy Block Houses V and VI

1 9 8 1

Toy Block Houses V and VI were created for an exhibit of housing models and were not intended to be built. For the exhibit, I designed two houses using a set of toy blocks, the Aida Block. I developed the set as a means of communication between an architect and his client. The participation of clients in the design process is becoming an important issue, and toy blocks offer many possible variations of residential spaces. I feel the development of this set also helped further my understanding of architecture.

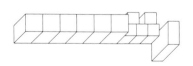 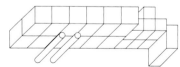 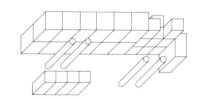

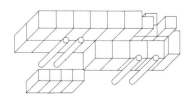 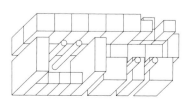 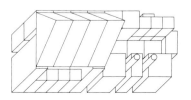

If the Aida Blocks represented architectural elements, they would be at the scale of approximately one to one hundred. Toy Block Houses V and VI explore the variations in houses that could be achieved with these pieces. Because these two houses use every piece of the set, they are larger than ordinary residential-scale buildings.

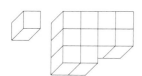

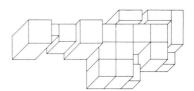

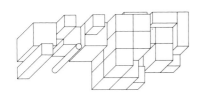
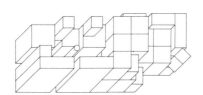
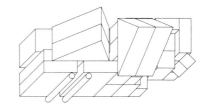

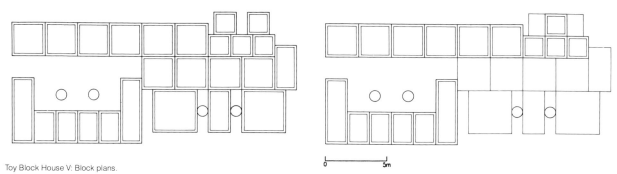

Toy Block House V: Block plans.

0   5m

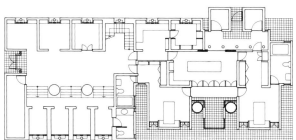

First floor plan.

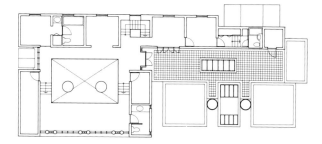

Second floor plan.

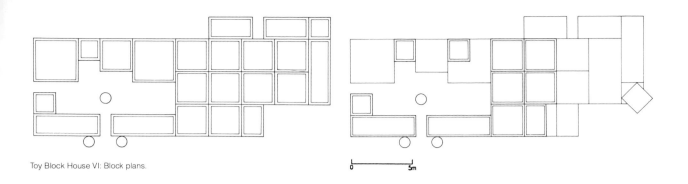

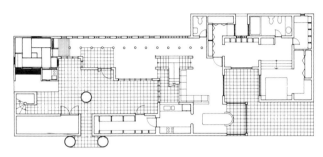

Toy Block House VI: Block plans.

0 —————— 5m

First floor plan.

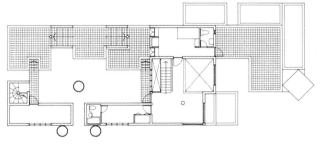

Second floor plan.

Toy Block House V axonometrics.

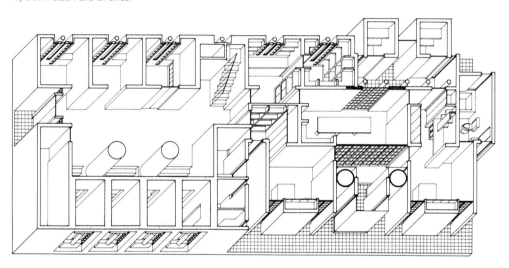

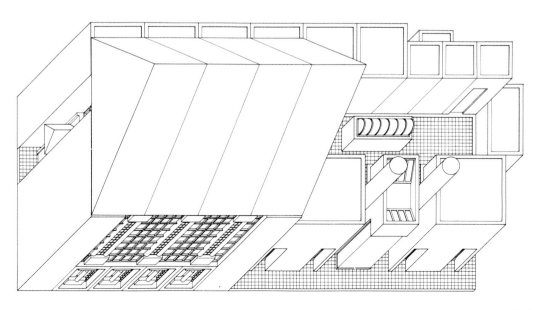

Toy Block House VI axonometrics.

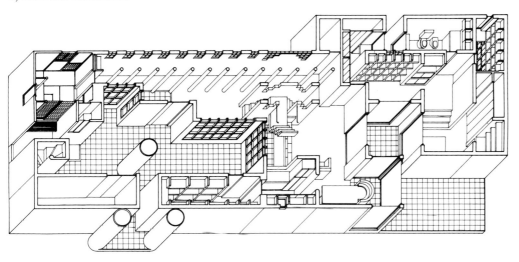

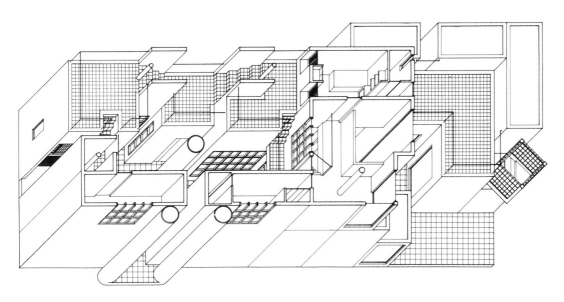

Toy Block House VII

1 9 8 3

In designing Toy Block House VII, I first had the idea of a box completely filled with toy blocks. Cutting the box and shifting its fragments creates interstices. These interstices develop into the required rooms. The exterior wall, given a coat of gray, metallic paint, appears like a box which has been cut and moved to reveal the presence of "toy blocks" that are actually white walls or openings.

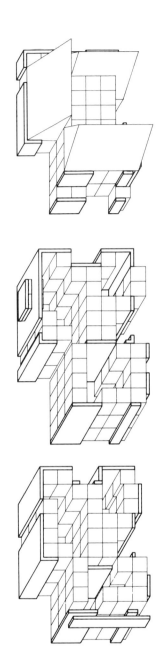

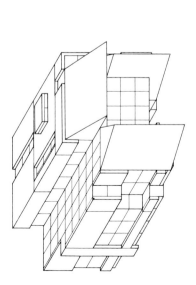

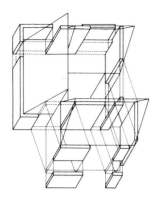

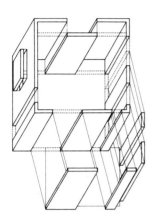

By cutting and shifting, I managed to articulate the facade and succeeded in giving this house a scale appropriate to the building's context, an area of small-sized dwellings.

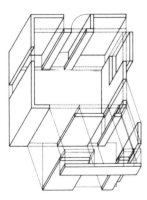

It is obviously difficult to transform a set of toy blocks, using all the pieces in the set, into an architectural space. However, one can become very absorbed in the procedure of trial and error; it is very much like being caught up in a game. Through the mediation of intellectual play, the architecture of toy blocks transforms into a "living architecture."

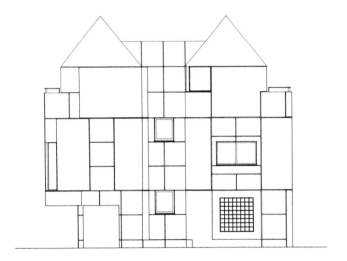

South elevation.

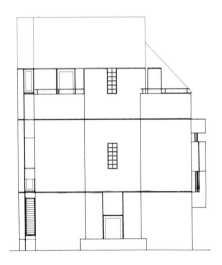

East elevation.

North elevation.

West elevation.

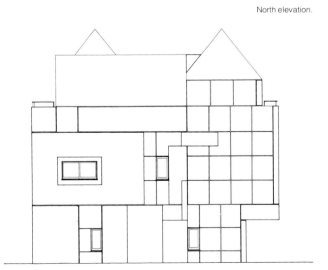

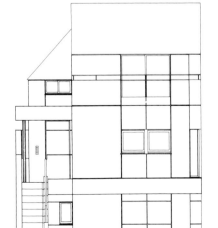

Right: view of south-east corner.
Below: south facade.

Toy Block House VIII

1 9 8 4

Toy Block House VIII began with two prototypical forms:
a cube and a cylinder. These two forms are each
composed of interlocking pieces; space is created by
gradually taking apart these pieces and in certain cases
destroying them. By repeated trial and error, the process
of space composition is reconciled with the process by
which the toy blocks are destroyed.

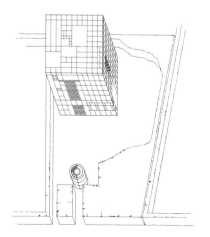
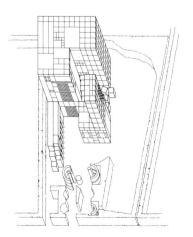
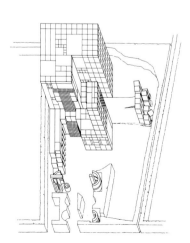

Here are two primary forms, a cube and a cylinder. The former is responsible for all interior functions; i.e., it provides such spaces as living room, dining room, and bedrooms for two families. The cylinder, on the other hand, is part of the exterior space; i.e., the approach and steps. This building is the result of mutual concessions on the part of the two primary forms and the displacements of individual pieces. In due course some of the pieces fall into the ground and are buried. The two extremes of destruction and creation here coexist. Even buildings that stand for a long time, like toy blocks, eventually may face obliteration . . .

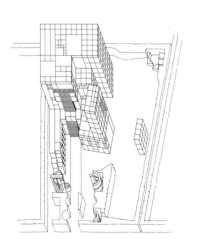 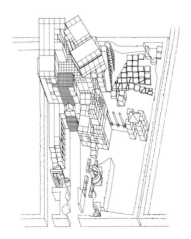 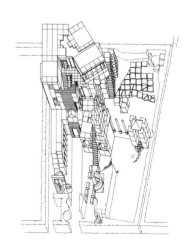

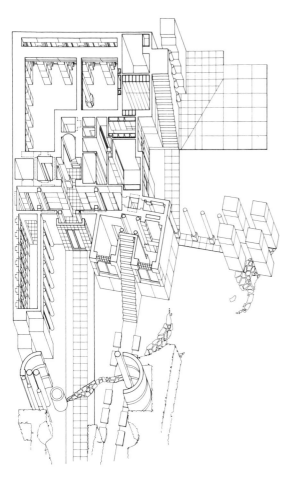

Axonometrics.

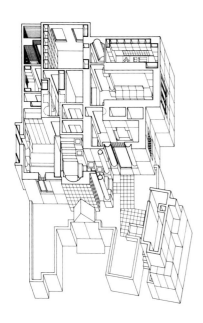

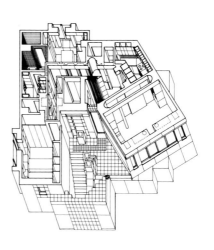

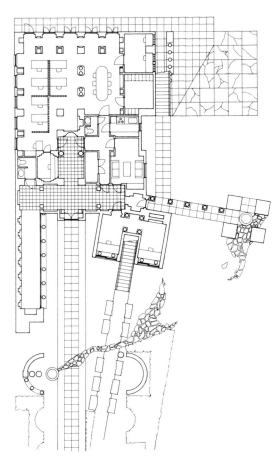

First floor plan.

Second floor plan.

Third floor plan.

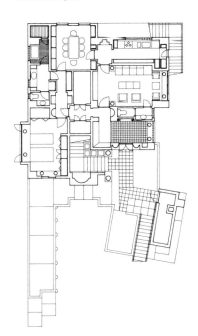

Toy Block House IX

1 9 8 3

The house consists of three rooms: a tea-ceremony room, a drawing room, and a dining room. These rooms are laid out to show the relationship between ritual space and daily activity spaces. The two zones have different surface materials and floor levels to emphasize the dinstinct spiritual nature of the tea-ceremony room.

The traditional Japanese structural frame allowed spatial interpenetrations between inside and outside. Four columns which symbolize the traditional frame and which make even greater interpenetration possible support the roof over the tea-ceremony room.

A fireplace stands in the middle of the house. Just as the *tokonoma* alcove is the symbol of a tea-ceremony room, the fireplace is the symbol of the daily activity spaces. It is the external symbol of the center of this house.

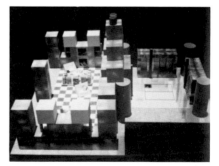

It is necessary to explain the composition of the traditional tea-ceremony room. *Tokonoma* is an alcove for the display of flower arrangements, ceramics, or works of calligraphy. The *tokonoma* developed, as the result of a long history, into the spiritual focus of a room. If one faces the *tokonoma*, there is an *oshiire* (closet) to the right and a *kazaridana* (niche) to the left. There is a hearth in the tea-ceremony room and, above it, a hook for hanging the *kama* (kettle).

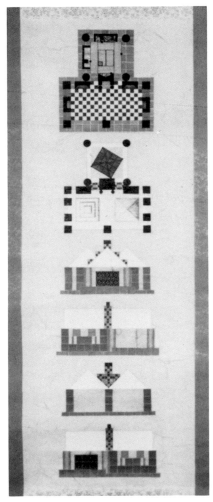

Toy Block House X

1 9 8 4

The idea behind the work is not the building up of toy blocks but instead their demolition or dissolution. This represents a further development of the "soft" mode of expression first used in Toy Block House III.

A box-shaped configuration of toy blocks is gradually destroyed. Pieces move from the northeast to the southwest, suggesting a flow, as blocks push outward to create interior space. Spaces shift while set-back regulations, natural lighting requirements, and the need for rooms of certain sizes are satisfied.

A sphere symbolizing the moment at which the process of destruction is halted stands in the center of this house. A momentary equilibrium between the forces of construction and destruction has been reached, and the sphere emphasizes the nature of this instant. The sphere in itself is a stable figure but expresses instability in the way it implies that it might roll off at any time.

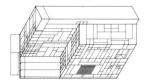
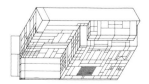
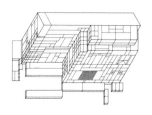
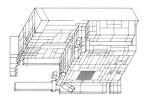

Entering a gatelike vestibule, one confronts a wall in which coupled columns emphasize the symmetry of the space. The vestibule and living room (defined by glass blocks) are composed symmetrically in order to give the structure a greater sense of reality as a building.

To the left of the vestibule, beyond the columns, a stair appears as an *objet* created from toy blocks. Ascending the stairs, one comes upon another sphere, a lighting fixture that symbolizes the center of the house. The sphere emphasizes the verticality of the stairwell and serves as the pivot of the interior space.

There are strong links between the plan, elevations, and sections, and the materials and colors used. The plan and elevation fixed the proportional relationship between the functions and flow of the forms. From the outside, it is difficult to tell that the structure is a supporting frame with walls set away from the columns and beams, thus creating a great deal of freedom in the design of the facade.

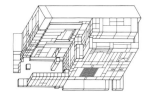 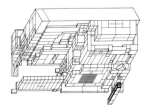 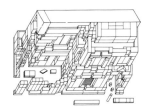 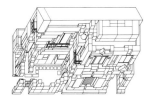

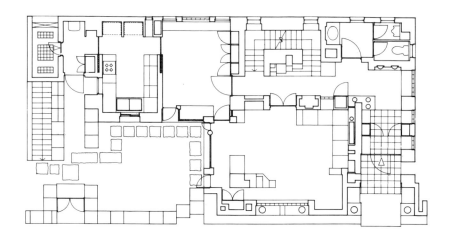

First floor plan.

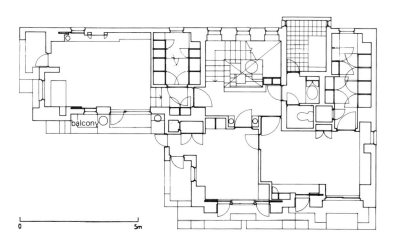

balcony

0   5m

Second floor plan.

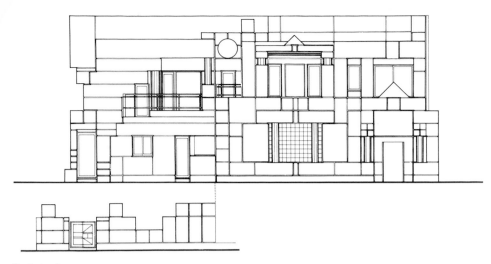

South elevation.

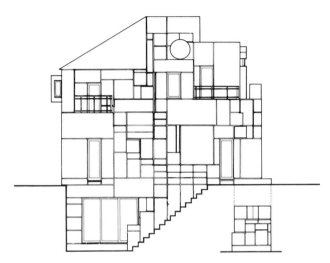

West elevation.

Section.

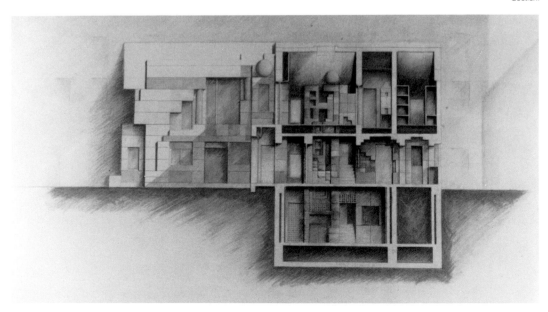

Preliminary sketches.

Studies for south-west court.

Left: west elevation.
Below: detail of south facade.
Opposite page: view up stairwell.

Nirvana House and Annihilation House

1 9 7 2

The basic design elements of both Nirvana House and Annihilation
House are square plan, symmetrical composition, and white walls. All of
these create a sense of things existing since ancient times. Both designs
attempt to imprison function within inherent forms. Furthermore,
I designed both houses to liberate architecture from function in order to
arrive at the innate idea-image of architecture.

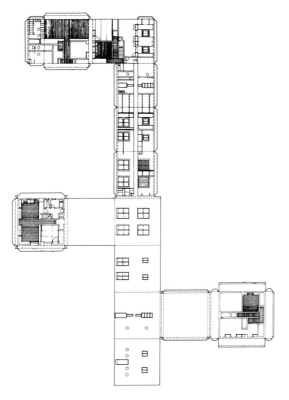

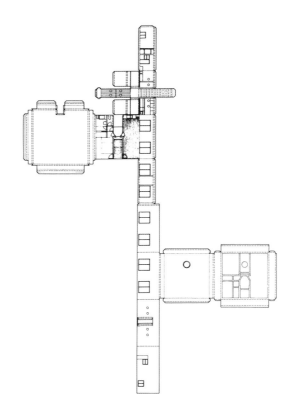

Okoshie Drawings.

Nirvana House.

Annihilation House.

Stepped-Platform House

1 9 7 5

I believe that symmetry can be divided into centrifugal and radiant types. This house is closer to the latter. Two axes intersect in the center: the entrance hall running north-south and the corridor running east-west. The entrance hall leads from exterior to exterior, and reveals the connection between the two blocks. The other axis leads from the living room to the master bedroom. The repetition of the stairstep motif in each terminal space of this axis amplifies the interior composition. Because of the symmetrical design, there is very little difference between the view from the living room to the master bedroom and the view in the opposite direction. Stairstep ceilings are visible from both ends, and the corridor is cut in the middle by the brightly lighted space of the entrance hall. Variations in the amplification of lighting, caused by the repetition of the stairstep form, produce an effect of involution.

The form is actualized when the stairsteps become a silhouette. It is impossible to overlook the silhouette effect created by the disappearance of details in the materials. The effect appears with the vicissitudes of time. The architectual silhouette is literally silence. But if the silhouette is the night face of the building, the architecture cannot tolerate temporary change unless it can adapt to the needs of a morning face. The more perfected the piece of architecture, the more profound the changes in its materials and forms from morning to evening. After about an hour of being bathed in evening winter sun, the gray-black of these slate walls deepens, and the silhouette of the building begins to manifest itself. At such times, the building seems to be even more a staircase form than it actually is.

Living room.

South facade.

House of Mondrian Pattern

1 9 8 0

House of Mondrian Pattern, as its title suggests, has as its theme a pattern by the artist Piet Mondrian. I played a game to see how a two-dimensional world might be translated into three-dimensional architectural space. The building plan was deived form Mondrian's "Rhombus: Colored Surface with a Gray Picture" (1919), and the site plan quotes a part of the pattern from his "Composition in Black, White, Yellow and Red" (1939-42).

Planning the house was like solving a puzzle. Mondrian's rhombic pattern was cut in half and the resulting arrangement was made to correspond to a house layout. The process, which kept to Mondrian's pattern for the most part, though allowed some slight departures from it, was almost enjoyable and similar to a game that required solving a succession of difficult questions.

I then developed the layout by converting Mondrian's pattern into a three-dimensional grid. In principal, a wall is installed wherever dictated by Mondrian's frame. Beams, columns, baseboards, and floors are painted metallic silver in order to make the grid apparent and to express its neutral character. Although it is a bearing-wall structure, columns are added to emphasize the grid. Transparent screens are used in the entrance hall to make the pattern more evident; the observer can see how in the center of the house the entrance hall, living room, courtyard, and *tatami* room relate to one another.

The design of the *tatami* room contrasts the grid derived from Mondrian's pattern and expressed by metallic silver paint with the unpainted, traditional wood members such as the *nageshi*, columns, and the *tokonoma* pillar. Creating unity from what are in a sense disharmonious elements is indeed an intellectual game.

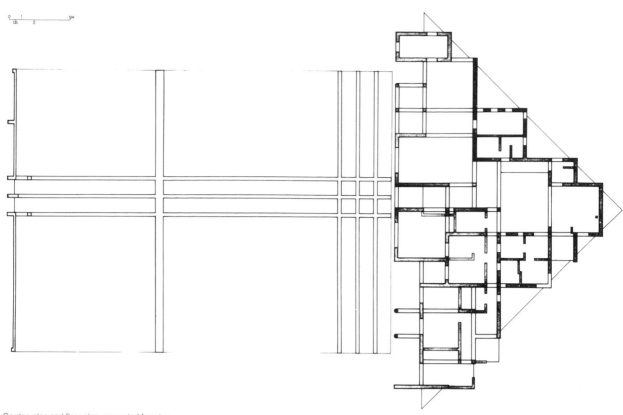

Garden plan and floor plan, generated from two
Mondrian paintings.

Axonometric.

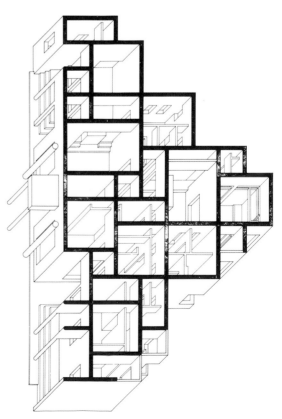

View of entrance door
from entrance hall.

View of dining room
from living room.

S House in Kitakaruizawa

1 9 8 4

The site is in Kitakaruizawa, in a resort development to the north of Mt. Asama. The land slopes gradually toward the northwest and is shaded by trees seven to eight meters tall. The sunlight barely trickles through the leaves in the summer, and the environment is relatively humid. At present, the only neighboring house is on the south side, but there is no guarantee that the site will remain this way.

These conditions result in the arrangement of the building proper in nearly the center of the site. Two parallel bearing walls are placed on the slope, oriented longitudinally with respect to the site, thus securing an interior space. Openings in these walls toward the north and south are kept to a minimum, and, in addition, lattices are used to provide visual buffers.

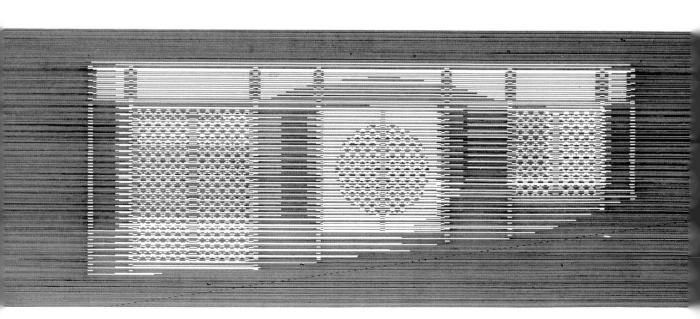

The rectangular plan is essentially a one-room composition. Byobu (screens) are employed as movable partitions because they provide flexibility. Following the slope, there are changes in the floor level and finish. The floor finishes, starting from the *doma* (working area), are local Assama stone, slate, paving block, wood flooring, and *tatami*, and progress from "hard" to "soft." The wash-basin in the *doma* and the hearth in the floored area are intended to provide a contrast of water and fire. Borderless, half-size *tatami* are placed in a checkerboard pattern, and the same pattern is used on the *shoji*.

The short side of the building facing the ravine is completely opened. This restricts the view outside, gives the interior space directionality, and promotes ventilation. The roof is pitched toward the ravine. The exterior lattice that envelops the building on four sides is designed as a membrane that makes the structure seem less massive and integrates the house with the surrounding woods.

North facade.

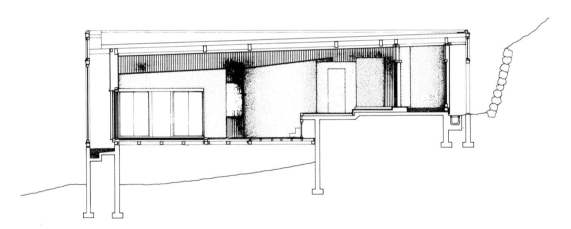

East-west section.

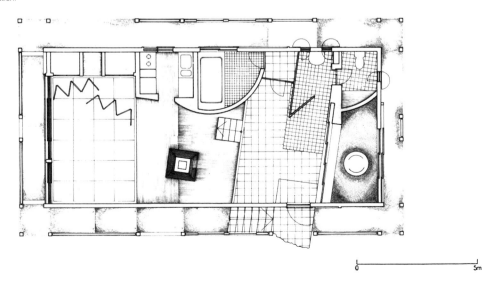

Floor plan.

0   5m

North facade.

View from *tatami* room.

Kajiwara House

1 9 8 7

The site faces a street of heavy traffic frequently encountered around provincial cities. Along the street are suburban restaurants, gasoline stands, used car lots, and many brightly colored billboards. Farm plots are scattered in their midst, and a range of mountains is in the distance. This site is typical of the area: a gasoline stand to the east and farmland to the west (this site, as well, used to be farmland). Its size is about eight meters north to south and fifty meters east to west.

Because of the site configuration and the location of the street, which runs along the south side of the property, I decided to arrange the planes along an east-west axis. By presenting the faces of the planes to the street, privacy is assured. In addition, the east-west axis exploits the form of the site, and produces effects of exaggerated perspective. The intention becomes clear the moment one stands in front of the glazed door of the main entrance. One sees through the entrance hall, past the corridor and lightwell, into the living room. Then one sees the outer wall of the child's bedroom (which is at a slight angle to emphasize its independence), the outer wall of the main bedroom, and the garden and areas outside the property.

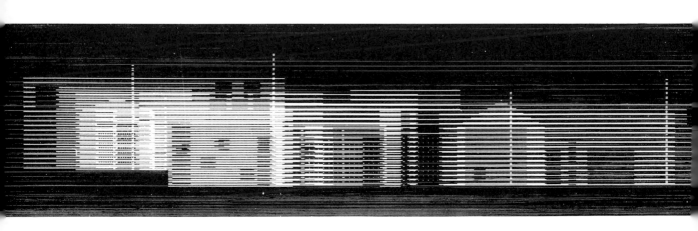

Uninterrupted views are provided eastward from each room. For example, the living room has a ceiling height of three meters and the aluminum sash on the east side is fixed so that the rails and stiles do not show. The result is an opening that is all glass and highly transparent. In the *tatami* room, perforated aluminum panels cover a ready-made aluminum *shoji* installed on the east side, and the effect is one of a floating screen. When sitting on the *tatami*, one can see across the lawn to areas beyond the property.

In the north-south direction, layered planes of different heights create effects of perspective. The drainpipes extend up into the air in order to make known the presence of more layers in the back. The openings made randomly in each plane afford views of the house and the mountains in the background and make the shapes of planes more ambiguous.

Glass blocks in the openings of the plane facing the street protect the house from noise. The aluminum *shoji* with perforated panels serve to assure the privacy of the courtyard and to frame the front garden, and also to communicate that this otherwise abstract set of planes is a house. The ready-made aluminum lattice door arranged diagonally in the front garden is also a vestige of residential architecture. Its light gray color renders the overall image ambiguous and causes the architecture to "fluctuate."

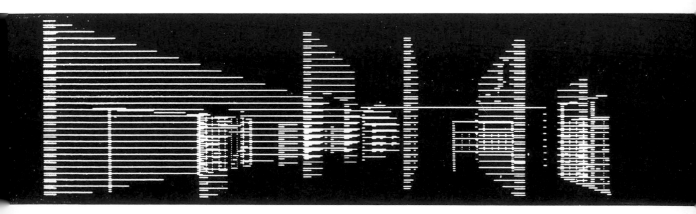

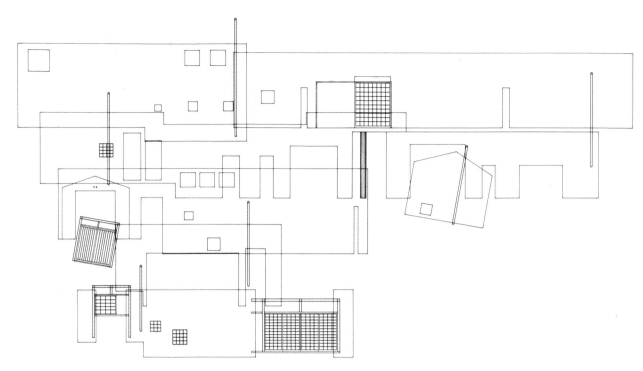

Concept drawing.

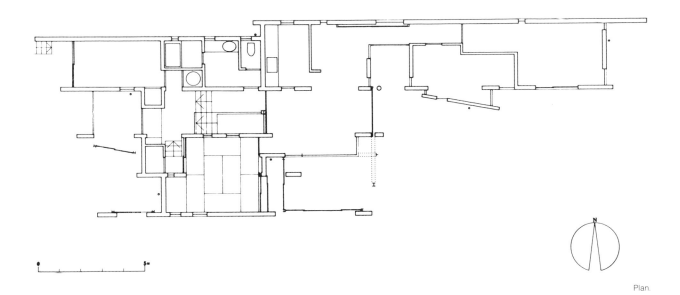

Plan.

View of model from south.

Opposite page: partial view of south facade.

Above: general view from south.
Below: view from south-west corner.

Kazama House

1 9 8 7

The site is surrounded by a mixture of old folkhouses, new tract houses, and farmland. Kawaguchi City's location across the Arakawa river from Tokyo, where land prices are so much higher, has prompted the gradual construction of condiminiums and houses.

The estates of the past have largely disapeared, but the site retains some of the atmosphere of an estate. A number of zelkova trees that are over fifty years old stand on the nearly 1000 square meter property, and a big cherry tree is along the street. The trees are important in that they attract birds and suggest the changing of seasons by their foliage. The client required to save the trees, moving them if necessary.

The clients are a couple with a grown child. The husband has an extensive collection of records and wanted to listen to them while looking at the trees. The arrangement of planes in the Kazama House is largely determined by existing trees and the street to the south of the property.

In order to provide unobstructed views of the trees, which are concentrated primarily on the east side of the site, the planes are oriented east-west (i.e., parallel to the X-axis). The spaces, each sandwiched between a pair of walls, create an exaggerated sense of perspective and emphasize the transparency in the direction of the trees in the garden.

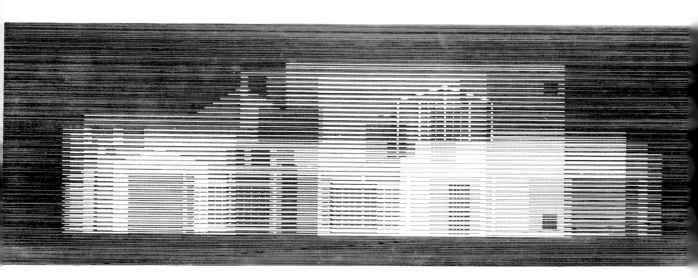

The clients also requested a southern exposure and a view of the large cherry tree by the street. A vista is provided, but in order to preserve the planar quality of the design, windows on the south are kept to a minimum. This assures privacy from the street and articulates a hierarchy of seclusion along the north-south axis (i.e., the Y-axis). The spatial layer nearest to the street contains the guestroom and living room. Seperated from it by a corridor is the next layer containing the kitchen, courtyard, and main bedroom. The layer containing the bathroom and toilet is beyond another corridor. Between layers, I introduced aluminum *shoji* covered with perforated aluminum panels to let interior and exterior spaces flow together.

Each plane is divided into smaller parts than in the Kajiwara House. In the interior, I deliberately raised those areas of the concrete walls that needed a finish—i.e., the parts that might come into contact with the human body or might draw condensation—by fifty millimeters. The result is a double-layered structure. To create a multilayered composition, I added house-shaped walls fifty millimeters outside the exterior walls. The *shoji* screens are not slid into walls but are slid behind the walls of the *tatami* rooms. Windows are created without relationship to the *shoji* screens. The two systems are independent, though contiguous. The *shoji* screens in the X-axis direction have been gridded in order to emphasize their planar quality; those in the Y-axis direction have only horizontal frames and are more translucent. Both the front door and the guestroom door are combinations of glazed doors and lattice doors, and whether they are pivoting doors or sliding doors is not made readily apparent.

The exterior walls in the X-axis direction are colored light gray, and those in the Y-axis direction are made white. By making the difference in value very slight and by creating openings, I have made glimpses of trees and the sky possible and have made the impression of the building ambiguous. In this way, I have sought to amplify the concept of "fluctuation."

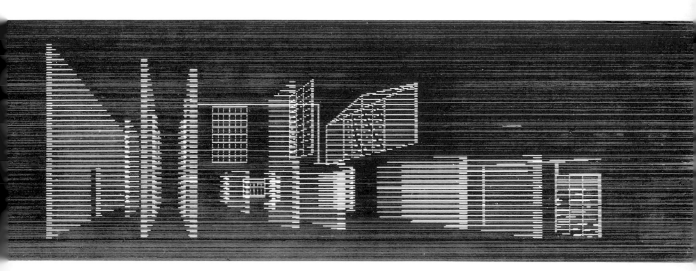

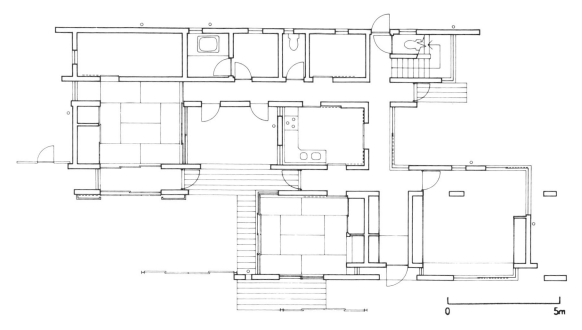

First floor plan.

View of model from south.

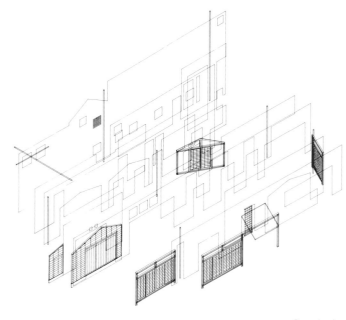

Show drawing.

Romeo and Juliet Castles

1 9 8 5

The main themes of the "Biennale of Venice" project are to trace the historical background of two castles, to create a new way to utilize the ruins, and to scheme out a phantasmic method of restoration for them. The Villa and Bella Guardia Castles have a romantic charm due to the celebrated work by Shakespeare, *Romeo and Juliet*. Converting this famed romantic story into an architectural methodology is our primary scheme.

The scheme is composed of:
1. 12 Months Performance, to link the seasonal variation with the composition of the stage;
2. Shadow of the Castles as they ought to be, to link the imaginary shadow (the shadow of the original form of the Castles) with the nature and sentiment of the story;
3. Pattern of the Japanese Playing Cards (*Hanafuda*: Flower Cards) to link the beauties of nature according to the Japanese lunar calendar with the composition of the stage;
4. Toy Block, to link the imaginary shadow and the composition of the stage methodologically and to create a playful atmosphere in and around the stage.

The drama of *Romeo and Juliet* is performed in each month throughout the year. In short, the story is divided into twelve pieces based on the main scenes. The titles are based on the key words of these scenes.

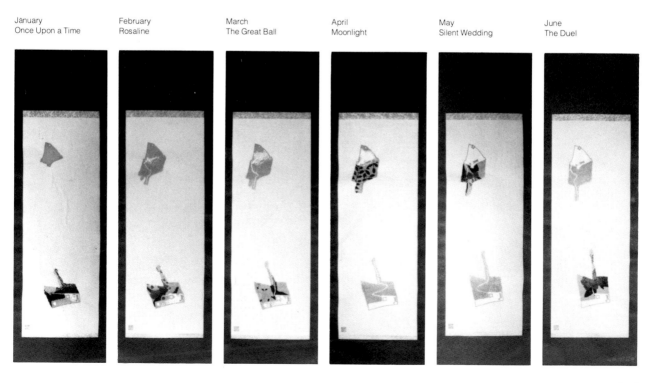

January
Once Upon a Time

February
Rosaline

March
The Great Ball

April
Moonlight

May
Silent Wedding

June
The Duel

The spot formed by the imaginary shadow of the Castles is assumed to be the area on which the stones of the original castle walls were razed and scattered disorderly. Stones in toy block shape constitute the imaginary shadow: the stage.

The evolution of the stage manifests the climax of the story. The stage for the performance from July to September is set either in the imaginary shadow of the "Romeo" or the "Juliet" Castle. The audience moves in accordance with the monthly evolution of the stage. The end of the story is performed in December, when the stage is set in the imaginary shadow of the "Romeo" and "Juliet" Castles simultaneously.

The stage alters itself twelve times in twelve months. The size of the shade expands toward the central point and becomes largest at the final phase of the drama performed in October and November. This illustrates the rise of the nature and sentiment of the play accompanying the evolution of *Romeo and Juliet*.

July
The Banishment

August
The Oath of Love

September
Agony

October
Grief

November
Death

December
And After

GKD Building

1 9 8 7

The GKD Building stands on a site on Futaba Avenue 300 meters west of the Shinkansen entrance to the JR Hiroshima Station. As in many other small and medium-sized cities, the area around the Shinkansen entrance is still not fully developed. A confused mixture of low and medium-sized buildings is around this site. Low-rise apartments belonging to the former Japan National Railway are across the street, and their dilapidated appearance, despite the abundance of greenery, adds to the area's backwater image.

In the near future, the entire area, including the extensive former JNR land, will undergo redevelopment. As a first step in this redevelopment, a huge and expressionless high-rise hotel has opened near the apartments. This heralds the random changes that will take place in the area in the future.

Futaba Avenue bends in the vicinity, as if to provide a view of the site from the Shinkansen entrance. As a result, the building's eastern and northern facades are easily visible from that direction. Moreover, one gets a very good view of the south elevation from a Shinkansen train coming into or leaving Hiroshima Station. From a visual point of view, the location is favorable.

Because of the environment and the location of the site, I decided to create a building whose design would serve as a nucleus for the improvement of the neighborhood. It is important that the building retain this role throughout the long process of redevelopment the area is slated to undergo.

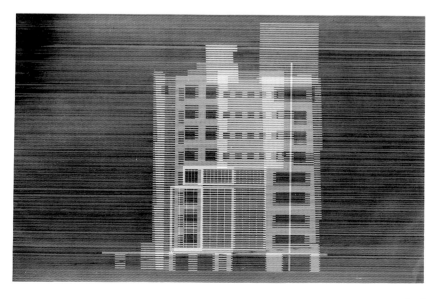

The building combines stores, rental offices, apartments, and parking. These different uses are included because there is a demand for tenant buildings in the area and because the site is located near the station.

The design intends to create a context different from the prevailing ambience, to suggest a new way in which the streetscape and the area in general could develop, and to provide the GKD Building with its own identity. In order to achieve this objective, multiple planar fragments, each endowed with a distinct image, are arranged in layers. This expresses the uneven and unstable process by which Japanese cities develop and provides an effective means of reinvigorating the area. Some planes are tilted and others are very orderly and independent. The *shoji*-like aluminum curtain wall and the huge aluminum lattice inserted among the planes are also distinct objects. The planes are in an unstable condition, and linear elements express both the horizontal and the vertical in order to demonstrate the intermingling of equilibrium and disequilibrium.

An observer has some difficulty immediately understanding the building's dynamic, the clearly defined and the ambiguous. This condition anticipates the future trend in the area. The building—which is within sight of what is likely to be the symbolic center of future redevelopment, the Shinkansen entrance—is like the mirage of a city that has never before been seen. The GKD Building embodies the idea of "fluctuation."

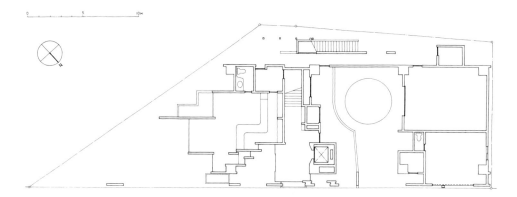

First floor plan.

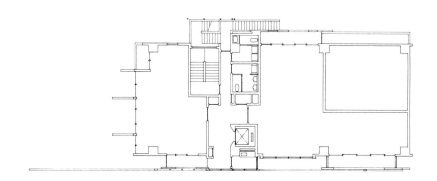

Office plan.

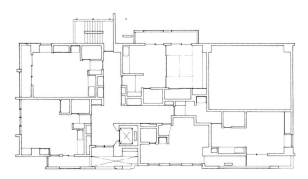

Housing plan.

North elevation.

South elevation.

Opposite page: view of model from north.
Left: south facade.
Below: view from north-east corner.

Temple Saionji Muryojudo

1 9 8 7

If I had to use one word to describe the concept behind my present works, it would be *yuragi* (fluctuation)—"a disturbance that nearly overturns the prevailing order but falls just short of doing so" or "a condition in which the existing order is transcended and a new system of a different dimension is created." The term "fluctuation" or "disturbance" was apparently first used by the chemist Ilya Prigogine. I am under no illusion that his theories have any direct application to architecture, but nevertheless they have been a stimulus to me in my work. The distance between architectural expression and language can never be entirely closed, but I believe it is possible to bring language closer to architecture and architecture closer to language.

Even as I spoke of the "playfulness" of toy blocks, I felt a growing discrepancy between my intentions and the resulting spatial compositions. I began to consider if it might be possible to create slightly "softer" toy-block spaces; i.e., to move from "visible" toy blocks to "invisible" toy blocks. This transformation is my present theme.

An "invisible space" is one that does not become visible until an observer consciously thinks about it. The creation of the space is left to those who experience it.

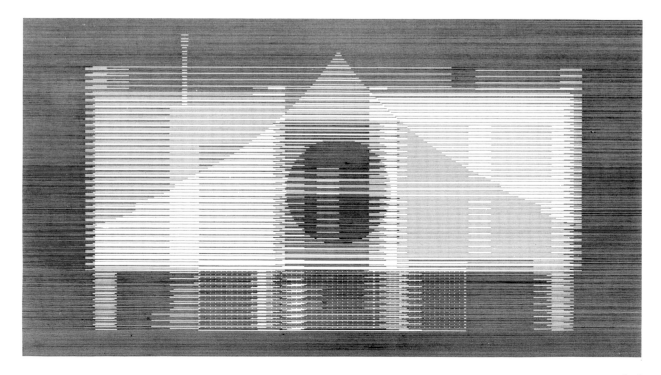

Architecture is basically three-dimensional, and that, reasonably enough, is the premise of architectural design. Nevertheless, it occurred to me to reduce space to two dimensions. I wondered if it might be possible to conceive three-dimensional spatial compositions such as interior spaces, each made up of walls, ceiling, and floor, and exterior spaces made up of roofs, exterior walls, and pilotis, in two-dimensional terms.

This means thinking as much as possible in terms of planes (such as walls and screens) instead of cuboids. The result is not two-dimensional or three-dimensional space. I could have called it 2.6- or 2.7-dimensional, but have tentatively chosen to call it 2.4-dimensional. To put it in a somewhat abstract way, this constitutes the fragmentation of dimensions. The intention is to heighten the effect of space by reducing the degree to which it is determined.

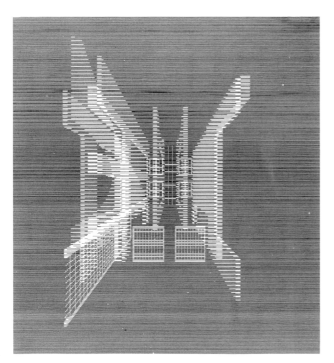

There used to be a series of samurai movies entitled *Hatamoto taikutsu otoko*. The climax was always the same: the hero dispatches one villain after another with his sword and finally confronts the head villain. A different set of *fusuma* screens was opened for each bit of swordsplay. The spatial composition of these movies was based on the planes of the *fusuma* and the changes in perspective. This was something like the effect of backdrops in plays. A change in backdrop can instaneously alter the scene on the stage.

The spatial composition of the Muryojudo is similar in certain respects to the planar world of traditional Japanese space and the world of backdrops. The following sequence is followed in layering planes from south to east:
1. the existing wall
2. a nameplate bearing the name of the temple, Saionji
3. a stainless steel mesh from which a (negative) figure representing the silhouette of the main hall has been cut
4. an exposed concrete wall
5. a lattice door
6. a stainless steel mesh from which a (positve) figure representing the silhouette of the main hall has been cut
7. an exposed concrete wall
8. a concrete wall with exposed aggregate
9. a nameplate
10. suspended and side walls of bush-hammered concrete
11. the same as above
12. an exposed concrete wall
13. a concrete wall with exposed aggregate
14. an exposed concrete wall
15. the gable end of the main hall.

The above mentioned planes are images or expressions of remembrance. The cut-out stainless steel mesh is modeled on the silhouette of the main hall roof. The silhouette is rendered in both positive and negative form, producing different planar compositions. Depending on the angle of light, the memory of the main hall may be awakened or erased. The hole in the center makes the main hall visible from the outside. The ossurary is integrated with the main hall by means of the symbolic name plate. At the entrance, one becomes aware of the presence of the main hall beyond the semi-transparent grating of the stairway.

In other words, three methods are used to make the observer conscious of the main hall: the cut-out silhouette, transparency, and semi-transparency. The layered planes endow the main hall with depth. If one looks at a cityscape through a telescopic lens, buildings appear to overlap and fluctuate—my intention is to produce a similar effect.

The composition of the planes is itself not compositional—perhaps it might be better described as anti-compositional or indeterminate. The planes approach order even as they fluctuate. I am attempting to produce spatial fluctuation while observing the minimum of rules, which in this case is to arrange the planes in parallel.

Saionji, a temple belonging to the Koshoji branch of the Shingon sect of Buddhism, is located in Sakaide City, Kagawa Prefecture. This ossuary of the temple is called the Muryojudo. The site of the ossuary is not very large, and, moreover, it does not go back very far. Arranging the existing wall, the *sanmon* (bell tower), and the main hall and moving the *jizo* (a guardian deity carved in stone) on the site proved very difficult. Another major problem was integrating the existing wood structure with the new concrete building.

The silent world of fluctuation is probably the same thing as the *gokuraku jodo* (western paradise) of Buddhism. I do not know what that western paradise is like, much less what an architecture that is expressive of its essence is like. However, one can try to discover that essence, bit by bit, though it may be a rash undertaking, like trying to capture one star from an infinite number of stars.

It is necessary to layer and transcribe images one by one: a *shoji* on which the shadows of trembling leaves are cast, foothills garlanded by the gauzy mist of springtime as in a *sumi-e* landscape, the waves, each one slightly different in shape and sound, a skyscraper made indistinct by haze. The Muryojudo is located not deep in the mountains, but in the city. It is hoped that the building will melt into the city while at the same time offering sudden glimpses of such images. The noise of the city has been accepted. The noise, the wind, the gaze of the observer, and the sunlight all overlap and create a space of fluctuation—one architectural response to the multifaceted and multilayered character of contemporary society.

Concept drawing.

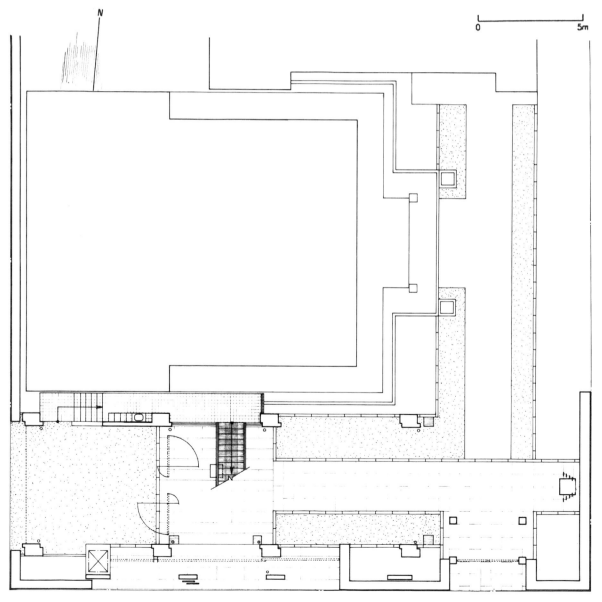

First floor plan.

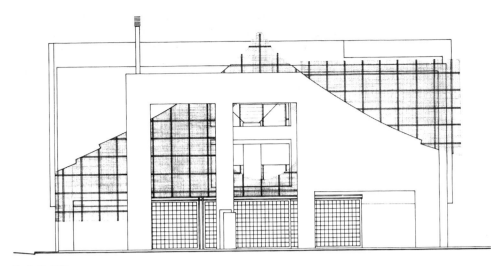

South elevation.

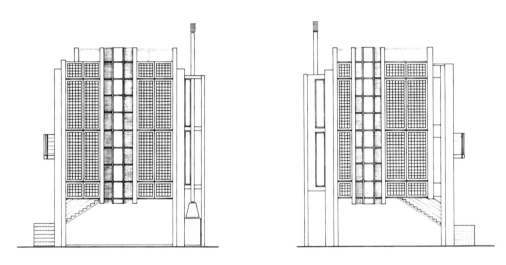

West elevation.

East elevation.

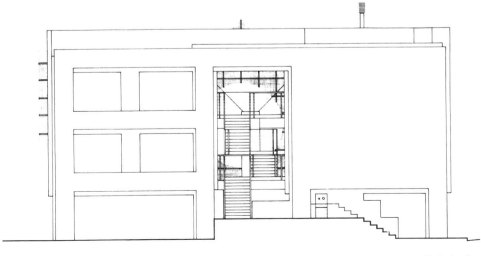

North elevation.

Tamatsukuri Hot Springs Monument

1 9 7 6

The Tamatsukuri Hot Springs resort is located off of a main highway in Shimane Prefecture. The city of Matsue is to the east, and Lake Shinji to the north. The major purpose of this monument is to act as a marker showing the location of the entrance to the resort and to catch the attention of travelers on the highway. My design takes this into consideration but provides a plaza as well.

In ordinary buildings, a work is born of harmony between and intertwinings of function and form. In a pure monument, there is no architectural function, and major attention is devoted to visual elements. In this case, my interest centers on two different approaches and their fusion. First, I adopted a deductive formal method of indicating the name of the hot springs: *tamatsukuri* means jewel making, and this region has been famous since ancient times for the manufacture of the curved, comma-shaped jewels called *magatama*. To indicate this, I represented the three elements of the ancient Japanese imperial regalia: the jewel, the mirror, and the sword. My second approach is the production of geometric figures. I set myself the problem of determining what geometric figures to use to relate the three parts of the imperial regalia.

Of course, there is inevitably an element of the arbitrary in the creative act. In my own work, for instance, both a fondness for symmetry and an attraction for forms that seem to belong to or derive from the setting are arbitrary. There must be, then, both the arbitrary and the nonarbitrary. In this case, I adopted a geometric approach in order to seperate in my own creative process the parts that must be arbitrarily determined from parts that must be determined nonarbitrarily. The geometric forms evolved on the basis of convention and according to fixed rules. Forms were determined automatically, and parts that might be the result of my personal will were eliminated.

I deduced the motifs of the jewel, sword, and the mirror geometrically.
I reduced these things to lines, spheres, circles, and vertically intersecting planes and expressed the relations among them in forms.

View from north.

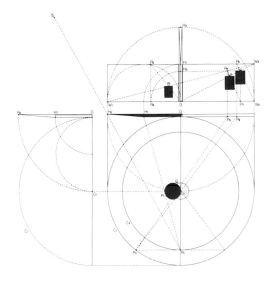

Reference drawing.

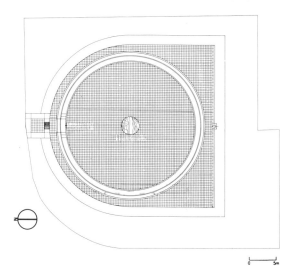

Plan.

The Memorial at Iwo-jima Island

1 9 8 3

The island of Io, known to Americans as Iwo Jima, was
the scene of one of the fiercest battles of World War II.
The Tokyo Metropolitan Government, under whose
jurisdiction the island lies, decided to raise a memorial
dedicated to peace and to those who gave their lives
there. People from many different fields held discussions
and made plans for the memorial.

The odor of sulphur, from which the island gets its name, is pervasive, but the place, far from
being desolate, is covered with lush vegetation. The task was to endow a junglelike site with
monumentality. The means employed are the establishment of an axis, the definition of a domain,
and the organization of a sequence of experiences. Another task was to express the theme of
dedication to peace and to the dead. The axis is directed toward Mt. Suribachi, the highest point
on the island, and along the axis a podium and an open space are located for those who come to
pay their respects. Four pillars define the boundaries of the podium and suggest its sacred
character. The memorial rises from a pool of water in the center of the podium. The open space
for visitors is defined by two pergolas that both close off and reveal the sky and impart to visitors
a sense of community. Movement, also, is an element in creating monumentality. Water from the
memorial flows through a channel under the pergola, past those who have come to pay their
respects, and, filling a circular pool at the end of its course, refreshes the flowering hibiscus.

As visitors approach the site from the parking area, they are confronted by the frame of the pergola. As they ascend steps, their eyes rest on a boulder marked by shelling. Once visitors are under the pergola, they glimpse Mt. Suribachi in the distance, and, against that background, the memorial and its reflection in the pool. Visitors offer flowers and then can look over the battlefield and read the plaques inscribed with poetry and a text explaining the history of the battle. They can enter the underground trench, a grim reminder of the fierce battle. This is a sequence of experiences that is meant to evoke memories and thus transcend what is immediately visible.

Tokyo War Dead Memorial Park

1 9 8 8

Regularity and symmetry are indespensable to
monuments, yet when these rules are applied too
rigidly, the result is an obviousness of composition
and a lack of resonance.

In the project, I use a symmetrical composition in the memorial park zone (in
order to express permanence) and make the path of movement
asymmetrical. A visitor always has the center of the open space in view. A
succession of gate-like forms are arranged along the path and, in the
manner of gates at shrines and temples, give space a sequential character.

As a consequence, the character of the place fluctuates
between the permanence of a monument and a
contemporary informality. Domains and boundaries
become ambiguous.

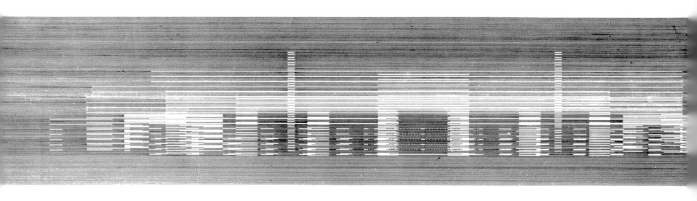

Another important theme in the manipulation of space is the relationship of architecture to exterior space. The overall composition is based on planes arranged parallel to two axes. These planes interpenetrate and conflict. In other words, the exterior space is not just leftover space; it is used to make architecture more outdoor in character, and the outdoors more architectural. This changes the fixed relationship between exterior and interior into a fluctuating relationship. In the memorial park zone, planes take the form of gate-like walls; in the rest area zone, the planes become fragmentary freestanding walls. Where necessary, floors and roof slabs are added to create interior spaces.

A number of words were in the back of my mind as I designed this project: life and death, regeneration and preservation, stability and instability, permanence and contemporariness, invisible context and clear geometry, closedness and openness, consciousness of the West and of things Japanese, architecture and nature. These pairs of ideas need to be united if we are to free ourselves of fixed notions in architecture. An architecture of fluctuation can help achieve such a unification.

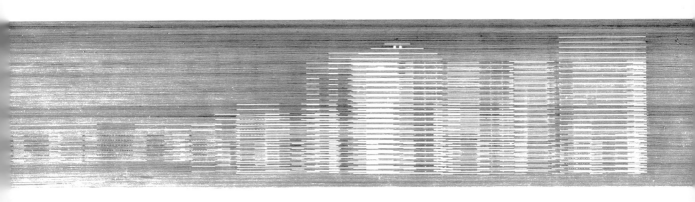

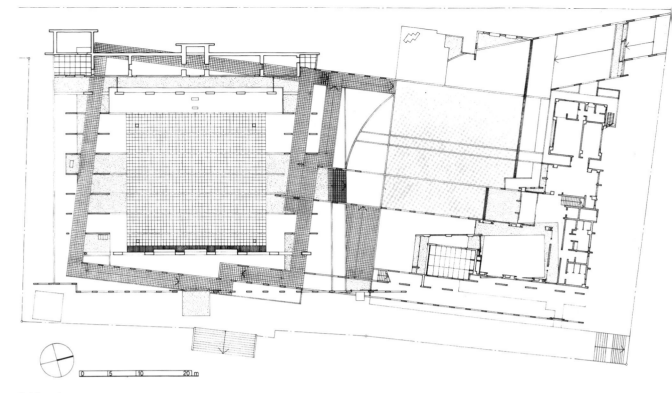

First floor plan.

South elevation.

East elevation.

North-south section.

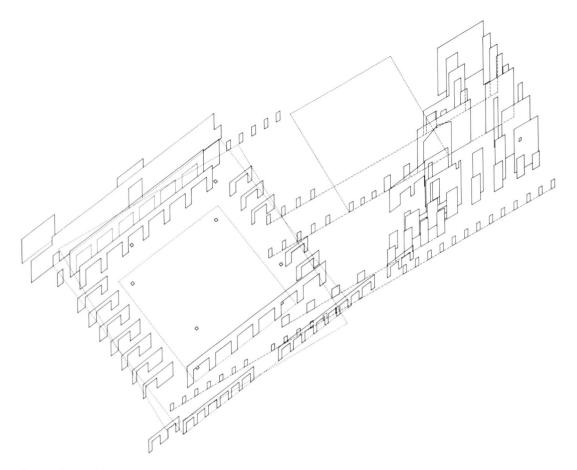

Conceptual axonometric.

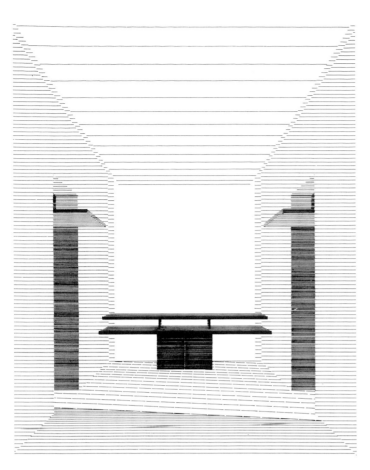

Yuragi drawings: interior of the crypt.

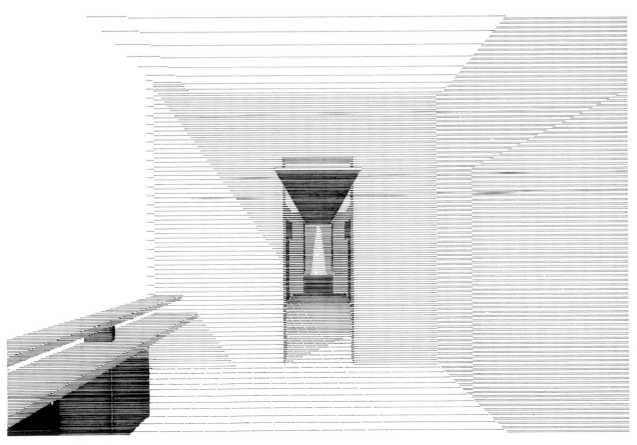

Above: layered walls of the rest area.
Opposite page
Top: view of model from east.
Center: view from north.
Bottom: view of plaza from west.

WORKS

1968 An Artist's House, Kunitachi, Tokyo.

1971 Anti-Avant-Garde House, Fujisawa, Kanagawa Pref.

1972 Nirvana House, Fujisawa, Kanagawa Pref.

1972 Annihilation House, Yokohama, Kanagawa Pref.

1972 Shike Showroom, Hodogaya, Kanagawa Pref.

1974 PL Institute Kindergarten, Tonbayashi, Osaka Pref.

1974 House Like a Die, Izu, Shizuoka Pref.

1974 Persona House, Suginami, Tokyo.

1976 Stepped Platform House, Kawasaki, Kanagawa Pref.

1977 Tamatsukui Hot Springs Monument, Tamatsukuri, Shimane Pref.

1977 Pension-Style Hotel at Shiobara, Shioya-gun, Tochigi Pref.

1979 Toy Block House I, Hofu, Yamaguchi Pref.

1979 Toy Block House II, Kawasaki, Kanagawa Pref.

1980 House of Mondrian Pattern, Kodaira, Tokyo.

1980 Live House Izumigaoka, Kanazawa, Ishikawa Pref.

1981 Toy Block House III, Nakano, Tokyo.

1982 Toy Block House IV, Suginami, Tokyo.

1983 Toy Block House VII, Meguro, Tokyo.

1983 Toy Block House IX (second prize—Doll's House Competition).

1983 Memorial at Iwo-jima Island, Iwo-jima, Tokyo.

1984 Toy Block House X, Shibuya, Tokyo.

1984 S House in Kitakaruizawa, Azuma-gun, Gunma Pref.

1985 The Romeo and Juliet Castles (project for Biennale of Venice).

1985 Shopping Center in Senpuku-Newtown, Susano, Shizuoka Pref. (ongoing project).

1987 Temple Saionji Muryojudo, Sakaide, Kagawa Pref.

1987 Kajiwara House, Ashina-gun, Hiroshima Pref.

1987 Kazama House, Kawaguchi, Saitama Pref.

1987 GKD Building, Hiroshima, Hiroshima Pref.

1988 Tokyo War Dead Memorial Park, Bunkyo, Tokyo.

PUBLICATIONS ON AIDA

Books:

1970 *Japan's Contemporary Houses 1.* Shokokusha, Tokyo.

1973 Rossi, Aldo, Franco Raggi, Massio Scolari, et al. *Architecttura Rationale.* Franco Angeli Editore, Milan.

1973 *Japanese Contemporary Architects 24 (Gendai-nihon-kenchikuka-zenshu 24).*

1973 *Gendai-sakka-shu 2*, Sanichi-shobo, Tokyo.

1973 Jencks, Charles. *Modern Movement in Architecture.* London.

1973 Fawcett, Chris. "Ontology of House." *GA Houses 4.* A.D.A. Edita, Tokyo.

1979 Drexler, Arthur. *Transformations in Modern* Architecture. The Museum of Modern Art, New York.

1979 *Jutaku-kenchiku-sekkei-rei-shu 5, jutaku to* Toppuraito 100 sen. Kenchiku-shiryo kenkyusha, Tokyo; An Artist's House.

1980 Jencks, Charles. *Late Modern Architecture.* Academy Editions, London, Annihilation House, Nirvana House, House Like a Die, and others.

1980 Jencks, Charles. *Post-Modern Classicism,* Architectural Profile; Toy Block House I.

1981 Seo, Tetsuo. *Toshi-Machi no Kenchiku, Architectural* Communication. Graphic-sha, Tokyo.

1982 *Drawings by Japanese Contemporary Architects.* Graphic-sha, Tokyo.

1983 Itami, Jun, ed. *A Collection of Drawings by 21* Japanese Architects. Kyuryu-do, Tokyo.

1984 Matsuba, Kazukiyo. *Japanese Post-Modernism* (Nihon no posto-modanizumu). Sansai-do, Tokyo; Toy Block Houses I, II, IV, VII, and VIII.

1984 *The Style of 2001 (2001 nen no Youshiki).* Shinkenchiku, special edition.

Articles:

1968 *Kindaikenchiku*, April; An Artist's House.

1968 *Shinkenchiku*, June; An Artist's House.

1971 *Kindaikenchiku*, June; Architext.

1971 *Sumai*, May; Anti-Avant-Garde House.

1972 *Toshijutaku*, August; Architext.

1972 *The Japan Architect*, August; Nirvana House.

1972 *Kindaikenchiku*, August; Nirvana House.

1973 *Toshijutaku*, December; House Like a Die.

1974 *Casabella*, January.

1974 Hasegawa, Takashi. *Shinkenchiku*, January; PL Institute Kindergarten

1974 *Shinkenchiku*, February; House Like a Die.

1974 *Kindaikenchiku*, March; An Artist's House, Anti-Avant-Garde House, Shike Showroom, Nirvana House, Annihilation House, PL Institute Kindergarten.

1974 *The Japan Architect*, April; PL Institute Kindergarten.

1974 Domus, June.

1974 *Kindaikenchiku*, April; Persona House.

1974 *Architecture D'Aujourd'hui*, November/December; House Like a Die.

1974 *Toshijutaku (jutakutokushu)*, special issue #7; Stepped Platform House.

1975 *Architectural Digest, February; PL Institute* Kindergarten.

1975 *Architecture and Builder* (South Africa), September; PL Institute Kindergarten.

1976 Honda, Kazuyuki. *Shinkenchiku*, June; Stepped Platform House.

1976 Jencks, Charles. "Architext and the Problem of Symbolism." *The Japan Architext*, June.

1976 *Space Design*, August; Stepped Platform House.

1976 *Bauen & Wohnen*, October; Stepped Platform House.

1976 *Shinkenchiku.* October; Tamatsukuri Hot Springs Monument.

1976 "Frammento Cosmologico." *Casabella*, #413; Stepped Platform House.

1976 *The Japan Architect*, December; Stepped Platform House.

1977 *Shinkenchiku*, March; Pension-Style Hotel at Shiobara.

1977 *Recherche & Architecture.* No. 29.

1977 *The Japan Architect*, March; Tamatsukuri Hot Springs Monument.

1977 *The Japan Architect*, June; Pension-Style Hotel at Shiobara.

1977 "Post Metabolism." *The Japan Architect*, October/November; 5 works.

1979 *Kenchikubunka*, October; Toy Block House I and House of Mondrian Pattern.

1979 *Shikenchiku*, October; Toy Block Houses I & II.

1979 *The Japan Architect*, December; Toy Block Houses I & II.

1979 *Shinkenchiku*, November; Live House Izumigaoka.

1981 *The Japan Architect*, March; Live House Izumigaoka.

1981 *Shinkenchiku*, June; House in Okubo (Okubo no ie).

1981 Takami, Kenshiro. "Mondrian Pattern; Sensed/Unsensed, Comments on the House Based on a Mondrian Pattern as a Metaphor." *Shinkenchiku*, August.

1981 *Domus*, No. 618, June; Toy Block House III.

1981 *Architectural Review*, September; House of Mondrian Pattern, Toy Block House III.

1981 *Parametro*, No. 99, August/September; House of Mondrian Pattern, Toy Block House III.

1982 "Free Style Classicism." *Architectural Design*, January/February; Toy Block House III.

1982 *Shikenchiku*, August; Toy Block House IV.

1982 *The Japan Architect*, November/December; Toy Block House III.

1983 *Techniques & Architecture* (Paris), March; Pension-Style Hotel at Shiobara.

1983 *Architecture D'Aujourd'hui*, April; Toy Block House I.

1983 *Architectural Design*, special issue on Doll's House.

1984 *The Japan Architect*, March; Memorial at Iwo-jima Island.

1984 *Architectural Digest*, May; House of Mondrian Pattern.
1985 *Shinkenchiku, jutakutokushu*, Spring; Toy Block House X.
1985 Davis, Douglas. "The Silent Generation." *Newsweek*, June 24 (U.S.A), July 1 (Japan).
1985 *The Japan Architect*, September; Toy Block House X.
1985 *The Japan Architect*, November/December; Toy Block House I, S House in Kitakaruisawa.
1985 Davis, Douglas. *Reader's Digest* (Japan), December; Toy Block House III, House of Mondrian Pattern, Nirvana House, Annihilation House.
1985 *Housing Review* (Japan), No. 11; Toy Block House III.
1986 *Toshijutaku*, January, pp. 49-51; Toy Block House IV.

PUBLICATIONS BY AIDA
Books:
1975 *The Theory of Architectural Forms (Kenchiku-keitai-ron)*. Meigensha, Tokyo.
1982 *Towards the Horizon of Architectural Forms* (Kenchiku-keitai no chihei wo motomete). Co-author Shin-kenchikugaku-taikei. Shoukokusha, Tokyo.
1984 *Architecture Note, Takefumi Aida, Toy Block Houses*. Maruzen, Tokyo.
1989 *What Kind of House Do You Feel Comfortable?* (co-author). Shoukpkusha, Tokyo.

Translations:
1971 Cook, Peter. *Action and Plan*. Co-translated by Yasufumi Kijima. Bijutsu Shuppansha, Tokyo.
1975 Mann, Roy. *Rivers in the City*. Kajima-shuppansha, Tokyo.
1983 Allen, Gerald and Richard Oliver. *Architectural Drawing: The Art and the Process*. Co-translated by Fumio Shimizu. Graphic-sha, Tokyo.

Articles:
1965 *Space Design*, April.
1967 "Approach to the Urban Residence, Symbol of the Urban Residence." *Shinkenchiku*, January.
1967 "Design Vocabulary, Sky Light." *Shinkenchiku*, April.
1967 "Urban Design Note: City and Factory." *Shinkenchiku*, October.
1967 "Possibilities of the Assembly of Factories." *Kindaikenchiku*, October.
1967 "Saikai Hyoryuki." *Kindaikenchiku*, November/December.
1968 Review of *Landscape Architecture*. *Kindaikenchiku*, May.
1968 "A Space of Encounters." *The Japan Architect*, June.
1968 Review of *Tabiji, Works of Imai Konji*. *Kindaikenchiku*, September.
1968 "Wall House: The Concept of Encampment." *Toshijutaku*, November.
1969 "Go to See the Sky of Europe." *Geijutsushincho*, February.

1969 "Can the House Serve as a Point of Origin? *Toshijutaku*, September.
1969 "Image of the House." *Kindaikenchiku*, September.
1970 "From a Polluted City to a Revitalized City." *Kindaikenchiku*, August-October.
1971 "Architecture as a Regard." *Kenchikubunka*, February.
1971 "What are the Techniques in Architecture?" *Toshijutaku*, April.
1971 "Is It Possible to Establish Rules in a City?" *Toshijutaku*, June.
1971 "Image of the House and a Model." *Kenchikuchishiki*, July.
1971 "Revitalized Architecture." *The Japan Architect*, July.
1971 "Movement Towards the Primary." *Toshijutaku*, September.
1971 "Plan for Box Houses." *Toshijutaku*, September.
1971 "Box-shaped Concrete Houses." *Atarashii-jutaku*, September.
1971 "An Open Environment." *Kindaikenchiku*, September.
1971 "Robert Venturi From Our Point of View." *Architecture and Urbanism*, October.
1972 "Anti-Avant-Garde House." *Kenchikubunka*, February.
1972 "From a Vertical City to a Horizontal City." *Kankyobunka*, April.
1972 "Lightness Intellectuality." *Shinkenchiku*, August.
1972 "Speculation in the Dark." *The Japan Architect*, November.
1973 "Leisure Theory of Territory." *Shinkenchiku*, September.
1974 "Takefumi Aida, 1964-74." *Kindaikenchiku*, March.
1974 "Twelve Memoranda on the House Like a Die." *The Japan Architect*, July.
1974 "When the Architecture Disappears." *The Japan Architect*, July.
1974 "Scenary—Even at That, Can the Architecture Continue Relating Something?" *Space Design*, November.
1974 "Forest Lawn Memorial Park and Mortuaries." *Architecture and Urbanism*, November.
1974 "From the Awe-inspiring the World of Sensuality." *Shinkenchiku*, November.
1974 "Function of Individual Housing: An Architect's View." *Kenchikuzasshi*, December.
1975 "From the Awe-inspiring the World of Sensuality" *The Japan Architect*, February.
1975 "Eliminating as a Method for Architectural Form." *Shokenshiku*, October.
1975 "Forms, Spaces of Silence and Calm." *Architecture and Urbanism*, December.
1976 "From Silence." *Architecture and Urbanism*, May.
1976 "About Silence." *Shinkenchiku*, June.
1976 "Concealment." *The Japan Architect*, June.
1976 "Form and Geometry (Keitai to zukei ni tsuite)." *Shinkenchiku*, October.

1976 "About Silence." *The Japan Architect*, December.

1977 "Forms and Drawings." *The Japan Architect*, March.

1977 "Between Silence and Loquacity." *The Japan Architect*, June.

1977 "My Esquisse." *Kenchikuchishiki*, November.

1977 "Silence." *The Japan Architect*, November/December.

1978 "A Good Architect is Born from a Good Client." *Nikkei Architecture*, February 20.

1978 "Silence: In the Culture of Sympathy." *Architecture and Urbanism*, March.

1978 "Silence." *Catalogue 10, A New Wave of Japanese Architecture*, September. The Institute for Architecture and Urban Studies, New York.

1979 "A Book I Was Inspired By." *Kenchiku Zasshi*, February.

1979 "A New Wave of Japanese Architecture Waving Back to the U.S.A." *Architecture and Urbanism*, March.

1981 "A Die Named Architecture." *Kenchikubunka*, July; a discussion with Kazuhiro Ishii.

1981 "On Playfulness." *Shinkenchiku*, August.

1981 "From the Lecture of Kenneth Frampton." *Kenchikubunka*, September.

1981 "To Unite Architecture With the Five Senses of a Man." *Nikkei Architecture*, September.

1981 *Kenchikuchishiki*, December; on House of Mondrian Pattern.

1984 "Toy Blocks, The Concept of Coexistancy of Construction and Destruction." *Architecture and Urbanism*, February; a discussion with H. Fujii and R. Miyake.

1985 Review of *Rekishi-Isho-ron* by Hiroshi Ooe. *Shinkenchiku*, May.

1985 "Tabino Tegami." *Shinkenchiku*, June-September; on a trip to China.

1985 "On Playfulness and Toy Blocks." *The Japan Architect*, September.

1986 "Something Hard." *Architecture and Urbanism*, September; criticism on Mario Botta.

1986 "Architecture of Arquitectonica." *Process Architecture*, February.

1986 "S House in Kitakaruizawa." *Architectural Design*, December.

1987 "Works of Takefumi Aida." *The Japan Architect*, May.

1987 "Kazama House." *The Architectural Review Japan*, November.

1989 "Architecture Fluctuation and Monument." *The Japan Architect*, February.

EXHIBITIONS

1973 "Triennale,"Milan.

1977 "Works of Takefumi Aida," Tokyo.

1978 "New Wave in Japanese Architecture," touring exhibition in the United States.

1978 "Today: An Exhibition of Houses," Tokyo.

1981 "Huset som billede, An Exhibition on Post Modern Architecture," Louisiana Art Gallery, Copenhagen, Denmark.

1982 "Exhibition on Seven Architects," Kobe, Japan.

1983 "Drawings of Japanese Architects," Space Art Gallery, Seoul, South Korea.

1984 "Architect's Drawings," Sagacho Exhibition Space, Tokyo.

1985 "Living in a Metropolis (Toshi ni sumu), exhibition on 13 architects born in the 1930s and 40s," Itabashi Kuritsu Art Gallery, Tokyo.

1986 "The Works of Takefumi Aida," John Nichols Gallery, New York, New York.

1986 "Exhibition of Contemporary Japanese Architects," GA Gallery, Japan.

1987 "The Works of Takefumi Aida," Ma Gallery, Japan.

1987 "The Works of Takefumi Aida," Tsubaki Gallery, Japan.

1988 "Exhibition of Contemporary Japanese Architects," GA Gallery, Japan.

PHOTO CREDITS

Masao Arai	pp. 5, 9, 14-15, 42-43.
Hiroshi Kobayashi	p. 91.
Mitsuo Matsuoka	pp. 47, 89, 98 m & b, 99.
Taisuke Ogawa	pp. 19, 45, 51, 55, 60-61, 66-67, 84-85.
J. Shimomura	p. 75.
Hiroshi Ueda	pp. iii, iv, 58, 65, 74, 83, 98t.

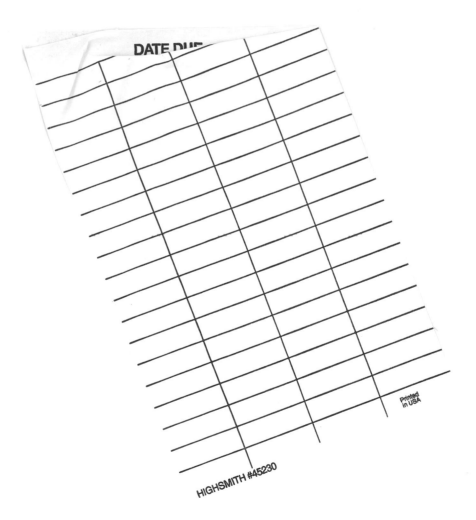

DATE DUE

HIGHSMITH #45230

Printed
in USA